Teesside

A book of short stories
from Norton and Stockton in the 1950s

By Alan Dodgson.

The author, aged 2½

RB
Rossendale Books

Published by Lulu Enterprises Inc.
3101 Hillsborough Street
Suite 210
Raleigh, NC 27607-5436
United States of America

Published in paperback 2017
Category: Family History
Copyright Alan Dodgson © 2017
ISBN : 978-0-244-60545-2

.

Contents

Teesside Tales

Dedicated to the memory of "Derek's" parents,
Kitty and Bill.

Thanks to Annette for all her help and advice.

The old believe everything, the middle-aged suspect
everything, and the young know everything.
Oscar Wilde, Writer and playwright.

Stockton on market day, c.1955
(public domain, stocktonteesside.co.uk)

Chapter One – Three Fishermen

Last year I went fishing with Salvador Dali. He was using a dotted line. He caught every other fish.
Steven Wright, comedian, writer.

Children played out every evening. Only heavy rain or freezing cold would stop them. After school, and after they'd had their tea, their first thought was to call for their best friends, and head outside to the back garden or street to play. They'd talk, laugh or argue about what they'd done at school then join with others for races or games along Waterford Road. There were no vehicles parking along the wide street, and only an occasional passing car held up the fun.

Footy was the most popular pastime especially for boys, though sometimes girls were grudgingly allowed – but only if they would go in goal. A makeshift goal was made on the kerb on one side of the road with old boxes or jumpers, and a goal on the other pavement. It wasn't very wide but if they wanted a wider pitch it meant going to the rec, a bit of a walk away. If the ball went over the fence into a garden, some hero would quickly scramble over the railing to collect it. It was only if it went over into old Moanin' Maunder's cabbage patch that there'd be a problem. Someone, and it was usually Dennis, had to be dared to jump over quick, before she came out and confiscated the ball. She appeared to have a sixth sense, somehow instinctively knowing when a football had landed in her cabbage patch, and made a beeline to retrieve it, and put an end to the match by amassing it with all the other confiscated contraband.

In the warm, balmy summer months there were lots more children playing out. Their parents were glad to get them out of the house, and for the most part they could check what was going on through the net-curtained windows or shout to them from the front door step. Derek's mam usually had her hands full with his younger brothers and sisters, and always told him to never go past the end of Waterford Road.

The days grew longer, and by midsummer it was light enough to play out until after ten o'clock. Dennis did stay out, but Derek and Micky were called in long before that. Officially bedtime was eight o'clock especially before a school day, but it could be stretched until nine if the next day was Saturday or a holiday. Lying in bed, the older kids' shouts could still be heard, playing chase or riding bikes along the crescent well after dark.

*****

Derek, Dennis and Micky could hardly wait for the long school summer holidays to come. It wasn't that they didn't like school, in fact Dennis Winter was a really good scholar, and he was always near the top of the "A" stream in Mrs. Gill's class. He was older than the other two by one school year, at Frederick Nattrass Juniors, and they always looked up to him. They weren't quite sure why he chose two younger kids to be pals with, even though he had lots of friends in his class.

Away from school the three lived close to each other, Dennis and Micky in Waterford Road and Derek in Clarendon Road just opposite. Dennis was the oldest and the smartest, and if anyone was the boss of their little gang it was him. To Derek and Micky he was worldly wise. He knew all sorts of stuff about all sorts of things and the young ones lapped up all that he had to share. Derek reckoned his astuteness had rubbed off from his two much older brothers who had already left the senior school. Vernon Winter worked at the Moderne Laundry in Norton, and brother Jack, who only just left school last year, worked as a navvy on that new estate in Billingham. Dennis was always arguing with them both, but especially with Jack who never seemed to have a good word to say to his younger sibling. The other kids in the street were scared of him and his bad temper, and stayed well clear of him in case he turned his wrath on them. Anyway, they weren't around much in the evenings, as they both spent much of their time in the pubs up in Norton.

*****

Kids in general, looked forward to the summer holidays to arrive! Six long weeks off were eagerly anticipated! Six weeks of freedom to do whatever they wished. The three pals met up in the gang hut on Saturday morning to decide what to do with their freedom; the gang hut was really Dennis's outdoor wash-house. His mam never used it though, except for storing half-empty paint tins and old rolls of lino. It was murky and damp inside. The concrete floor was grimy and the brick walls messily white-washed. The only light came from a two-foot wide wooden window that was permanently stuck shut as the damp had warped the wooden frame. Above you could see the rafters which were covered with black slates on the outside. There was no electricity, but there was running water and a large, square porcelain sink and a wooden draining board. In the corner was a corroded wash tub with an old wooden posse, neither of which had been used in years. As a headquarters it was ideal, as Dennis's mam preferred to go to the launderette once a week, and if they kept reasonably quiet, nobody would disturb them.

Dennis usually took the lead. "I wouldn't mind going to Billy Bottoms to see if we can catch owt." Billy Bottoms was their name for the Billingham Beck, a narrow but deep and gently flowing brook, a tributary which eventually fed the River Tees. There was a play park on the banks, and plenty of places to dip your net.

"Yeh, I've got loads of jam jars but I haven't got a net," answered Micky enthusiastically.

"I'm not sure if me mam'll let us go," Derek cut in tamely.

"Well don't tell 'er – say you're going to the rec'," Dennis said, forthright in that always-assured voice, suggesting everything would be fine.

"Me mam won't be bothered, I'm supposed to be at me Auntie Jean's," put in Micky, "but I'll just say that I'm playing round at yours." There was only Micky and his mam living at their council house for as long as the others could remember. No-one seemed to know where his dad was, and no-one ever spoke about it – that was just how it was. During school holidays, and holy days of obligation, Micky was farmed out to his mam's sister's house in Raleigh Road, whilst she went off to work at the shop. But Auntie Jean had four kids of her own, all younger than Micky and she was more than happy to let him play out on his own. Micky didn't go to the same school as the other two. He went to St. Patrick's Juniors by The Green. He was a 'Catlic', whereas Derek and Dennis were 'Proddies' – yeah, that's 'Catholic' and 'Protestant'! They were a little bit jealous of Micky as he always seemed to have lots more days off school than they did.

The three agreed the plan of action. They would set off after dinner. Before that they had to get the jam jars ready, with pieces of string tied around the necks for carrying, and repair the nets and replace the bamboo canes if necessary. This took most of the rest of the morning, searching for string and pinching old canes from the garden shed, before Dennis left for some dinner, and Derek went home with Micky in tow.

"Mam, can Micky have some dinner here?" Derek asked.

"Where's yer mam Micky?" came the reply.

"Oh she's at work in the shop." Micky timidly answered.

"Aye oright sit yourselves down – you can be first." Despite having a load of kids of her own to feed, she had a soft spot for Micky and was happy to feed him. Derek's mam knew that Micky wasn't looked after that well, though she never said so in front of the kids.

The lads tried valiantly to keep things out of sight, but Derek's all-seeing mam clocked that something was going on. "I hope you're not going down to Billingham, our Derek," she said whilst stirring a huge pan of steaming soup on the gas hob (*why did she always make soup in the middle of Summer* ?!).

Derek's mam, Kitty, c. 1950.

"No Mam," he lied, "we're going up the rec and then to the duck pond."

"Aye well, you two mind what you're doing – and stay with Dennis." He even seemed to have a reassuring effect on adults. Derek seemed to have got away with it, but still felt guilty for telling lies to his mam. He comforted himself by saying it was only a small fib, and that anyway he was helping her by 'getting out from under her feet' as she always said to his Dad.

*****

Straight after chicken broth and dried bread, the three pals met up, and set off on their afternoon adventure. They put the glass jars in Dennis's army surplus backpacks along with a lemonade bottle full of drinking water. The nets on canes, doubled as swords, turning the boys into warriors engaging in imaginary battles. They headed up Drake Road, through the back streets, along the Blacky Path, on past the village shops then up Norton Road to The Green.

By now the July afternoon had become really warm, and the boys' three jumpers soon found their way into Dennis's bag along with the other stuff. The Green was teeming with kids playing games, and milling around the duck pond on this, the first day of the six-weeks-off. Some big lads were playing footy and younger ones were with their mams feeding the ducks and pigeons.

The Green and duck pond, Norton.

Some babies or toddlers were being wheeled around in Tansads by young teenage girls who'd been charged with minding them for the day. A few little ones wearing bathing suits were running about on the grass or paddling in the pond, whilst older folks sat around the Green on benches or under the shade of the huge oak tree, keeping an eye on the kids and watching the world go by.

The two younger boys were sorely tempted to stay. "Look at all these!" shouted Micky, "I've never seen so many here before." It certainly was busy, the little shop and the two ice-cream vans were doing a roaring trade. The good weather on this first day of the school holidays had brought people out in droves, and there was sure to be a few sunburned the next day.

"Come on let's go," said Dennis clearly much more interested in the next leg of the journey than staying. And so they walked on, past the blacksmiths yard and across the Village Green by the Red House School and into Mill Lane. It was here that their odyssey really began. They crossed the lane and onto a side track which the boys knew as Tarzan's Trail. They soon left the few houses behind on one side and looked across to golden wheat fields on the other, stretching into the distance. Before them was a narrow and shaded clay path weaving its way through poplar, willow and oak trees, surrounded by dense bushes and shrubs.

"You wait here for a minute then come and find me!" Dennis shouted over his shoulder as he sprinted ahead along the Trail. The other two obeyed, counting in tens to 200, giving Dennis ample time to hide before they set off to search for him. There were plenty of hiding places on both sides of the Trail, and Micky and Derek gingerly tip-toed along, hoping not to be ambushed before they found him.

But Dennis was too wily for them. He waited until they had walked past his hiding place by a large badger sett opening. "Ahaaa! Gocha!" as he leapt from behind. The others groaned then giggled, sorry to be caught out so easily. "Your turn Micky," said Dennis and Micky ran off to hide.

The hide-and-seeking continued for the next half a mile, each taking their turn, until they emerged into a clearing, and they excitedly looked down upon a small valley through which Billingham Beck gently meandered.

ICI Billingham works.
(public domain, teessidepsychogeography.com)

The backdrop to the beck was the mass of factories and plants of the ICI chemical industries – hundreds of meandering pipes, scores of tall chimneys belching smoke and goodness-knows-what chemicals to pollute the already smog-laden atmosphere. The stench of ammonia and the reek of hydrogen sulphide pervaded the air.

*****

Despite the sun being its hottest now, the three friends simultaneously broke out into an easy jog, down the slope and across the ancient wooden footbridge to an old and deserted kid's playground. Only two swings out of six were working, but the indestructible see-saw and the rickety roundabout still worked well enough.

They lost interest in the play-park as they exhausted themselves and sauntered off to follow the thin grass path by the beck. "Shall we go to the Secret Spot?" Micky asked the others.

"Yes, it's easily the best place to catch something," answered Derek. Dennis agreed and they walked on for a hundred yards, to a bend in the beck which they regarded as their own special fishing spot. The outside of the beck's meander meant that their side was fairly deep whilst the other side was shallow. The beck itself ranged between twelve and twenty feet in width and of undetermined depth in the centre. At the edges the depth varied from a foot or so where they could see the bottom, and deeper parts where the water was a lot murkier. There was a flat grassy area by the bank at the Secret Spot, and they were all able to stand there to dip their nets. They were after tadpoles, frogs or newts but the real prizes were minnows, delicate silver fish less than a couple of inches long, and the slightly larger stickleback, with its red under-belly and prominent spines on the dorsal fins. They'd seen bigger fish in the beck before, like pike and roach, but the boys thought that these were out of their league, and left them for the anglers with rod-and-reel that they occasionally saw on the bank.

"No! Not like that!" Dennis called to the others as they eagerly shoved their nets straight in, "you'll stir up all the mud, and we won't be able to see anything!" But it was too late, so Micky moved further along the bank and Derek further in the other direction. The bottoms wandered gently that day, after a long period of sunshine and no rain. The bank sides were mostly dry yet still muddy and slippery in places. Micky found a clearer place to fish, and his first dip brought up nothing but weed, which he placed in a jam jar and topped it up with water. Derek found a clear spot and peered into the depths to search for the prize catch.

"Hey! Quick!" It was Micky – what had he seen? The others looked up just in time to see Mickey's head disappearing from view as he slipped down the steep banking! Dennis and Derek leapt up and sprinted back along the beck path. They arrived to see Micky stood waist high in water, dripping wet. "Aaah! Get me out!" He'd managed to find the muddiest, slipperiest bit of banking, and promptly slipped down it as he reached in with his net a catch a minnow.

"Quick, grab this!" shouted Derek and he thrust his cane towards Micky. He gratefully held it as Dennis pulled him the few feet to the shore. It was still difficult to clamber out, as the sides were steep and now covered in water from the splash, but somehow between them, Dennis and Derek managed to drag Micky up and over the edge to the top of the banking. Micky was absolutely soaking from head to toe, his t-shirt and pants caked with mud, his face was filthy and he had bits of weed on his head and shoulders.

"You were lucky it wasn't deep," said Dennis.

"I know. Me mam'll play war – she'll go mad!" replied Micky as he stood before them dripping, shivering and smelling of Billingham Bottoms mud.

Dennis let out a small giggle. "Shurrup!" came Micky's indignant response. Derek joined in the giggling. "Eeeh look at me!" Despite Micky's misfortune, the giggling changed to gentle laughter, and Micky's grimace changed to a grin as he began to see the funny side.

The three continued their fishing despite Micky's drenching, reasoning that it would be better for him to suffer the wet discomfort, whilst the sun dried him off, rather than risk the wrath of his mam or auntie if he returned home soaking.

They passed the rest of their time peering into the depths, searching for places where aquatic creatures might hide, and gently dipping and wafting their nets. The peaceful summer afternoon drifted on, only periodically pierced by excited cries from one or another, when a catch was made. Newts, snails, and worms were in abundance. Fish were harder to locate, harder still to catch. Frogs were plentiful though they were all unsure whether they were frogs or toads.

When they began to grow weary from their efforts and the sun's heat, they came together to total up their bounty. The final count was eight frogs (or toads?), two newts, seven water snails, twelve worms, two minnows, and the prize-catch, which the wily Dennis netted, a two-inch stickleback with a beautiful red under-belly and two spikes on its back.

Stickleback
(public domain, flickr.com)

They decided to let the newts and frogs go. They liberated them, placing them on the bank and watched as they made their way back to the beck and freedom. The minnows and stickleback would be kept as trophies, each in their own jar along the with a few water snails, some worms and pond weed. When they got back they'd be kept in the gang hut in Dennis's old goldfish bowl.

The three, finally exhausted, began the return journey along Tarzan's Trail. It was much less energetic, as each had jars of fish or beck water to carry. They'd drank their shared bottle of drinking water long since, and were soon feeling thirsty again. The majority of people and kids at the duck pond had drifted away home for their afternoon tea. The exhausting trudge through the final streets leading to home continued with little conversation, the boys realising that the adventure for this day was almost over, and thoughts turned to what tomorrow would bring.

Chapter Two – Budding Entrepreneurs

One must be poor to know the luxury of giving.
George Eliot, writer.

Dennis seemed to know all the best tricks for making money. Maybe it was because of what his elder brothers had taught him from all of their dodgy dealings. Dennis was the brightest of the Winter clan though, and he not only gleaned all of *their* tricks, but conjured up many of his own too. It wasn't so much that Dennis and his friends, Micky and Derek, needed money, as they never had money of any great amount for themselves before, except for the odd sixpence from an aunty or uncle, or for a birthday gift.

For their first business venture, Dennis's idea was to follow a set route around the local streets to collect empty lemonade bottles. The overall plan was to collect the bottles and return them to the grocer's shop. You see, each time a bottle of Lowlock's Lemonade was sold, the cost included a deposit of 3d, so that the manufacturers were sure to have their bottles re-cycled, as the 3d deposit was reimbursed on the return of the bottle. The thing was, the majority of people would either forget to take their empties back when they went to the shops, or they couldn't be bothered, and a pile of empties would simply grow outside their back door.

Those who weren't very well off couldn't afford lemonade in the first place. Either that or they took their own bottles back. So Dennis's scheme was to go to the posher people's houses – to knock on their doors and ask if they wanted their empty lemonade, orangeade or cream-soda bottles returned. After all, Dennis reasoned tongue in cheek, the boys would be doing a public service for the community, by helping to clear unwanted 'rubbish', and not merely lining their own pockets!

The plan worked a treat. Business boomed! Oh, everyone knew that, in effect, the boys were begging, but most were glad to see the back of their empties, and reckoned it was worth 3d to get them removed, and that it would save them having to carry them all the way to the Avenue shops.

The next part of the plot entailed bottle transportation, because they believed that the number of empties would soon grow. This is where the two younger boys were able to contribute. Derek had a 'bogie', and so did Micky, and they were both commandeered into action for the new business venture. Derek's dad had helped both of them make the bogies. This entailed using a plank of wood, 5 or 6 feet long, and the wheels and axles from an old pram. If you were cheeky enough, you could get these for nothing, by simply asking the scrap yard man. The front and back of the plank needed the wheels attaching, and this is where a dad came in useful – someone to show the boys how to attach the rear wheels to the plank, and how to attach the front axle so that they could steer the whole thing – needing a hole to be drilled and a large nut-and-bolt centred through the plank. Finally, a loop of string or old skipping rope was fixed to both sides of the front axle, to steer the bogie, or to be towed.

The boys used their bogies to play on, to race up and down the street or to take it to the rec where there were a couple of good sized banks to run down. The latter could be quite perilous, as there was no device for stopping the bogie! The best way was to leave a foot dangling out of the back, and to drag it along the ground. Trouble was, it didn't exactly ingratiate you with your mam if you came home with a hole in the sole, or worse still in the leather upper, especially if it was your pair of school shoes or, in Micky's case, your only pair!

So then, the bogies were drummed into service for their new job and, with a large cardboard box from the off-licence placed securely on the back of the plank, the bogie could comfortably tow as many as thirty or so lemonade bottles at a time.

A posh bogie, c. 1955
(public domain scottishcarties.org.uk)

The boys set off around the Albany Estate together. Dennis made sure they got into role by wearing some of their poorer clothes, so as not to look too well-off and just a little impoverished – patched-up short trousers, a ragged shirt and a holey, sleeveless cardigan. At first, it was Dennis who knocked on people's doors, and asked, politely, if they had any lemonade bottles that they didn't want. Sometimes the people said no, and sent them on their way, and some said that they had, but would return them themselves. Occasionally, some said that the boys could take the bottles back if they gave them a penny per bottle back, though most gave the bottles willingly.

The latter group fell into three categories. First were the ones were either lethargic or lazy, those who couldn't be bothered to return the bottles and claim the deposit back. Secondly, there were those who were old, frail or feeble and found it difficult to carry the bottles any distance, and so were glad for someone to have their back step cleared. These were the ones that the boys felt most sorry for, but still took their bottles! The third group were the philanthropists – those who felt that they were doing their civic duty by helping their poor fellow man (or in this case their fellow boys) in some small way – especially when they looked at the three abject wretches in front of them, or studied, with some sympathy, the piteous looks in their eyes!

Micky and Derek studied Dennis's performance and followed his lead on how to knock on doors, what to say, and even how to say it – with cheerless and pathetic voices. The results of their playacting and labours proved to be very fruitful. With just an afternoon's work, the boys had filled their bogies with no less than seventy lemonade bottles. When they appeared at Frederick's Grocery, the shopkeeper was taken aback, to say the least, at the number of bottles that had been collected, but accepted them, and then had to find space in his own backyard, to store them until the weekly drinks lorry returned.

Mr. Frederick was usually reluctant to hand over a deposit for just one bottle, and now he grudgingly had to open his till and hand over the deposits for all seventy bottles! Seventy bottles at 3d per bottle came to a grand total of 210 pennies, or seventeen shillings and six pence – no wonder Mr. Frederick had looked so disconcerted!

To the gang though, this was tantamount to a small fortune, and afterwards in their den (...really Dennis's mam's wash-house) they sat, smiling and staring at it – an orange ten-bob note, two half crowns, two shillings and a silver sixpence. They could hardly believe that this was theirs, and pondered on how just a few hours work could be so lucrative. Of course, some of it would be given back, as the boys had promised some of their 'customers' a penny per bottle when they'd taken them back. Dennis had kept a note of the addresses where money was to be returned, but after these 'overheads' were dealt with, that still left them with a handsome profit of 15/6d !

They were rich! But what to do with their earnings – after all their efforts, they didn't want to waste it or fritter it away. Guided by Dennis's suggestions, and agreed by all, they decided that each of them would join the Fireworks Savings Club at Jenson's hardware store. They'd each save two shillings, and later add some more when they could. By the time Bonfire Night came, they should have plenty of savings to buy some decent fireworks, bangers and sparklers.

Sparklers!
(public domain pinterest.com)

Next, they'd invest some of the money into buying full bottles of lemonade, store it in the den, and then sell it to their customers, and make a small profit for the delivery charge! Best of all they could spend some of their earnings on luxuries for themselves – on a Basset's sherbet fountain, a packet of Spangles, Jubblies, comics or even a bottle of lemonade! Derek said that they should each give their mam some money to help with the family food bills. They all agreed that it was a good idea to keep them happy. It proved to be a very good suggestion and, even though they didn't reveal the full extent of their endeavours and profits, when each mother was handed one and six pence, they were so delighted that they immediately gave a three-penny bit back to each boy to keep for himself!

The next afternoon, the three budding businessmen set out again, just as the day before, but this time to South Road in Norton. Dennis knew that there were some big houses there, each containing posh and probably rich people. They knew that the gardens were big, as they had all been there, in the dark, last harvest time, when they helped themselves not only to apple and pear windfalls, but plenty off the trees too!

The result was the same as the day before, but this time their net profit was a little down at fourteen shillings and four pence – maybe really rich people weren't as philanthropic as others ...? Nevertheless, once again they felt as rich as princes, and promptly disposed of the money in the same way – some to the Firework Club, some to their mams, and with the rest, they gorged themselves on sweets and pop. This day though, the mothers all became a little alarmed with their boys, and wondered if there was something amiss in what they'd been doing. Each boy was closely cross-questioned, and each one managed to convince their mother that there was nothing untoward. Even so, to be fair to the parents, they were more concerned that their boys should be enjoying the school summer holidays while the weather was good, rather than roaming the streets, and getting up to who-knows-what sort of trouble, or into what sort of danger.

But the lads were not to be put off that easily. They weren't fed up with what they were doing - after all, it *was* work of a sort, and not play. Yes, they missed their footy with the others at the rec, and rides around the streets on the bogies, but since they'd seen the colour of real money, they'd become a little mesmerised with it, and ached for more of it! There'd be plenty of time for play later.

On their third day of work, they all agreed to say nothing to the mothers, except that they were going to the rec to play. This time though, they travelled a fair distance to the Roseworth estate, and on the journey took turns, to be pulled along on one of the bogies. Once again, Dennis had planned the route that they were to follow for the afternoon.

Just before the knocking on the first door, all three of them turned to the sound of a truck, stopped dead, and stared in disbelief towards the bottom of Roseneath Avenue! There, coming towards them, and pausing at each house in turn, was a Lowcocks' drinks lorry! Two workers manned the lorry, and the boys quickly realised that not only were they selling lemonade, but collecting empties and returning deposits as well! They were all astonished and completely deflated at what they were gawping at, as each of them realised that this meant that their new business venture was about to be nipped in the bud, before it had barely begun!

Dennis, in particular, was smart enough to perceive that this was a small glimpse of the future – it was just a matter of time before the Lowcocks' lorries would be everywhere, and who would want to give away their empty bottles for re-cycling then?!

The boys knew that they couldn't go back to the same estates as the previous days, as the pickings would be meagre for at least a couple of weeks. For the next couple of days, they tried some other estates where Lowcocks hadn't yet ventured, but began to realise that their hearts weren't really in it anymore, and turned away from the world of commerce, and to leave it to the grown-ups. In any case, the Firework Savings funds were looking pretty healthy now, and as the August sun continued to beat down ever more brightly, they yearned for the rec – to take a spin on the roundabout, to play on the swings, to ride the witch's hat or to play a game of footy with their pals.

The witch's hat.
(public domain, dailymail.co.uk)

Chapter Three – Trespass

There are three ways to get something done: do it yourself, employ someone, or forbid your children to do it.
Monta Crane, writer and teacher.

Derek's council house backed onto the railway line, a single track line that stretched from the Stockton sidings to the factories at Portrack, the steelyards at Haverton Hill, and the docks and refineries along the north bank of the River Tees. At least two trains every hour passed Derek's house, from early morning until late in the evening. Sometimes, the engines were old steam-shunters, but more often lately, they were newer diesel locomotives, which were much more powerful, and were able to tow a lot more wagons. These diesels pulled the large, heavy fuel, oil and coal wagons, whereas the steam trains' rolling stock was longer, and carried iron and steel girders or heavy-duty machinery and chemical fertilizers.

The chuff-chuff of a steam engine or the hum of a diesel could be heard long before its appearance. The screech of metal on metal, as the locomotive rounded the bend gave warning of the imminent arrival of a terrifying monster. As it passed Derek's house, the noise rose to a crescendo, especially if it was a steamer with a heavy load, chugging along at a snail's pace. But living with the noise, day-in day-out, Derek had got used to it, as had everyone whose house backed onto the railway line.

Kids adored the smells of the steam engines, the oils lubricating the shafts and pistons, and the acrid stench of smoke belching from the beast's coal furnace. Not so the housewives though, who came to curse the engines – especially on a Monday, the traditional day for washing and drying the family laundry. It wasn't so much the smoke that bothered them but the after-effects – when tiny airborne particles of ash and soot floated down to settle on clothes-horse and washing line.

Kids too, loved the awesome fierceness of the massive locomotives. On hearing the brute approach, Derek and his brothers and sisters would run to look through the railings. It was always a delight if the engine driver waved back at them. Each one counted the wagons and compared answers when the train had passed – the most they had ever counted was thirty seven trucks. There was always a guards-van on the back, yet seldom a guard to be seen. "He's probably inside having a cup o' tea from his flask," their dad would say.

The kids were warned on pain of a slapped leg or a thick ear, never to cross the railings or to go near the track. Even so, the blackberries growing between fence and track proved too much of a temptation for Derek and Dennis, and if Derek's mam wasn't about, they'd climb over and gorge themselves on the biggest and most sumptuous of the berries.

There was a dirt path, just over the railings, which ran along the fences. Some adults used it to take a short-cut towards the dog track at Tilery, or the walk to Stockton. It snaked along the backs of several of the council houses, for about two hundred yards, first along the flat, then along the top of the cutting, to the bridge at Norton Road. To get onto the road, there was a large wooden gate with an enormous metal spring to ensure that it closed by itself. Sometimes, it was a short-cut used by Derek and Dennis too.

The friends knew that the track was strictly forbidden to them, how perilous it could be and how obstructions on the line could derail a train – but in some strange way, it was that danger which attracted them, and the need for sharp pointy metal for their arrows! Dennis figured that if they put just a small object on the line, it wouldn't cause a problem for the engine. They'd experimented already with an old ha'penny. Before the train's arrival, Dennis had leapt the fence and boldly, if tentatively, approached the line and sat the coin in place on one of the rails. They watched with some trepidation, to see if their antics would cause the train to be derailed, but found that the tiny coin was no match for the colossal locomotive. When the train had gone, the coin was collected – it had fallen from the line and squeezed by immense pressure, into a thin, shiny metal disc, still hot to the touch, with the king's head completely obliterated!

They soon graduated to bigger objects, the largest being six-inch nails that Micky had found rusting in his wash-house. The work of the engine's wheels left shiny, flat, pointed nails, which were ideal (not to mention lethal) for tying onto a bamboo cane, and using as a spear or with a bow for toy fights. One such fight ended when an arrow hit Derek on the bridge of his nose, perilously close to his left eye, and piercing the skin. The amount of blood flowing from his head terrified the boys, and since that incident they'd all become a lot more chastened. The arrow left quite a scar – half an inch long – which stayed with Derek well into adulthood.

*****

Despite those dire warnings, Derek still climbed the railings to explore what was over – the dirt path one way, gardening allotments the other. He'd seen men passing, using the short-cut going to and from the allotments. Even his dad used the path to go to the bookies down Norton Road.

They'd seen the warning notices before of course, emblazoned with the legend, *'Trespassers will be Prosecuted'* but they always thought that it was just to warn people to keep off the tracks. One of Derek and Dennis's escapades onto the railway was when they ventured towards the sidings, on their way to the market in Stockton. There was a place where the tracks criss-crossed; some tracks went off east towards Middlesbrough and Redcar, some north towards Hartlepool, and others went to join the main line to Darlington. The sidings were run down, not at all what they used to be, as much of the business in rolling stock had moved elsewhere. A lot of the rails were rusted over; some had been taken up completely and laid on the side, along with piles of redundant sleepers and stacks of iron clasps and holders. There were two disused signal boxes and several dilapidated workmen's huts.

The trip to the railway sidings took less than ten minutes. They walked by the side of the track or hopped along from sleeper to sleeper, always alert for the sound of any approaching trains - those new diesel Deltics could be really quiet! If one did come they'd smartly hide in the bushes by the side of the track until it was safely past.

They were intrigued by the old signal huts, and curiosity got the better of them – they had to look inside. Some were locked or bolted, others half open with doors or windows hanging off hinges. Inside there was little of interest – some had battered wooden tables, or the odd chair or stool. Some of them were clearly used as nothing less than latrines for track workers, where a hole in the ground had been dug. Even though they hadn't been used for some time, a stench of urine and faeces still lingered and hung in the air.

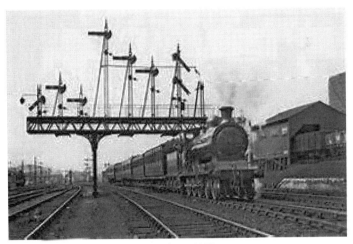

Signals, c. 1955
(public domain, lightmoor.co.uk)

The disused signal boxes held much more attraction. Much of the glass had been broken and the doors were ajar. Inside, they still had all the levers that had been used for changing the signals for all of the routes away from Stockton. By now the newer signalling systems were beginning to take over, leaving the old boxes open to the elements to decay. One had a clock high up on the wall, and an old, black, but disconnected telephone on a side table. On the walls were torn railway charts and maps, faded brown with age. The boys would pretend to be signalmen, pulling levers and phoning ahead to the next box, whilst all the time looking out, in case a driver from a passing train should spot and report them.

The final part of the trip to town was a five-minute walk – along an embankment, then leaving the track through a gate near the Head Wrightson's steelworks offices, on Norton Road past Tilery. After town, this was the way back, past Tilery Rec, maybe to play on the swings or watch the old men playing bowls on their immaculately manicured flat greens.

It was about the third time that they'd taken this route to town. As they rounded the bend to reach the old signal boxes, they spotted two figures approaching on the track from the opposite direction. The two lads walked on, outwardly feigning indifference. "Just keep walking, they're just two fellas using the short cut as well," whispered Dennis. But their hearts were thumping, and their heads reeling with a mixture of anxiety and excitement. What else could they do … to turn back now would make them look stupid, or simply be an admission of guilt … they would keep walking and bluff it out.

As they came closer, the boys could see that the men were dressed in normal street clothes — shirts, dark jackets, trousers and heavy black boots. Were the boots a give-away? But in their heads, the lads were just going to carry on and say nothing. The younger man stopped with a friendly, "Hello!" He had a kindly face sporting a thin moustache, with well-groomed, Brylcreemed hair. "I'm Detective Constable Porter and this is Detective Constable Jeffries," he continued.

The boys were rendered speechless, and felt their feet and legs turning to stone. They were unable to move, and their hearts pounded even faster. They could barely believe what they were hearing – maybe it was the calm and friendly voice that had at first lulled them into a false sense of security, or maybe it was just some sort of silly trick that the men were playing. Oh yes, they'd heard about the railway coppers before from older lads, but they imagined them in uniform with big helmets and a truncheon!

"Sit down over here on the bank will you lads, so I can ask you a few questions?" said the first policeman, now with a little more authority. The boys began to realise that this was no ruse, that the game was up, and they meekly did as they were told.

The second policeman now took over, speaking just as calmly, and opening a small black book to take notes. He told the boys that they were being charged and prosecuted with trespassing on railway property, and said that they didn't need to say anything unless they wanted to. He asked each boy the same questions in turn, starting with an enquiry about what they were doing on the railway. Dennis spoke first, saying that they were taking a short-cut to Stockton. Derek repeated his answer word for word. Then the policeman took down their names and addresses.

The first policeman took over again, finishing the interview by saying that someone would be calling on their parents in the next few days. The two men escorted the boys to the nearest railway crossing where they were told to make their own way home by road.

*****

Dennis still couldn't believe it! And even if it was true, they wouldn't prosecute them anyway, he told Derek, it was all just to scare them, just to tell them off! They decided not to tell their mams and dads, instead to wait and see if anything else happens.

But it *was* true! Two days later, early in the morning, there was a heavy knock on Derek's front door. His dad had gone to work, and Derek and mam holding the baby, went into the parlour, with the very same two detectives. Afterwards, she was a bit more than upset, and clearly saddened, and barely knew what to say. Derek too, was upset, suddenly full of remorse, as he felt the huge weight of guilt hanging over him. The inquest would begin in earnest when his father got home; in the meanwhile, Derek was to stay indoors for the rest of the day, find something to do, and not get under her feet.

To Derek's amazement (and relief!), his dad was somewhat pragmatic about the whole episode – what was done was done! He was an intelligent and logical man, and saw no good in ranting and raving at his son – indeed he was quite the opposite – calm and reasoned in his questioning, and rational with his reprimands. It would do no good to cry over spilt milk; rather he had to consider how to deal with the problem now. Derek felt that, for now at least, he'd got off lightly. His dad felt that any further admonishment would be hypocritical, since he too, in using the railway path as a short-cut, was equally guilty of trespass.

When he finally got to talk to Dennis, days after the dust had settled, Derek found out that the same scenes had taken place in his house, and that his dad had been round to see Dennis's dad. He had overheard the conversation, which had got a bit heated. Derek's dad had accused the older boy, for leading his boy on, and Mr. Winter blamed Derek, saying that it was because their house was right next to the railway, and that he should be watched more closely! The men had calmed down on parting, and decided to wait and see, and hopefully the case and the charges would be dropped.

The hope was a vain one. Three weeks later, each family received a postal summons to appear at the Juvenile Court in Major Street, at 10 o'clock on the 24th September.

*****

There were ten children altogether; all boys, all of a similar age. They were told to line up in front of the bench. Derek and Dennis were in the middle of the line. The bench consisted of five middle-aged people, four men and one woman. They were all finely adorned and groomed, and each stared impassively at the line of offenders before them. The side seats of the Magistrate's Court were reserved for the public, though for this hearing there was only the parents of the boys. On the other side, there was seating for the press, that day just one young reporter. Behind the boys there was seating, desks and pews for court officials, solicitors, council, for social services and the police.

There were two clerks, a stenographer, and two court bailiffs who marshalled the ten young criminals. At the very back sat two uniformed policemen.

Derek and Dennis wore short trousers, a shirt and blazer, short grey socks and black shoes - effectively their Sunday best. Six of the other boys were similarly dressed and the other two wore long trousers, shirts and ties. Even Derek's dad wore a shirt, tie and suit for the court appearance, something which he rarely did. From the sombre looks on their faces, none of the dads were overjoyed to be there, most of whom had had to negotiate a morning off work, and worse, suffer the loss of half a day's pay.

The lead magistrate, seated at the centre of the bench, nodded to the senior bailiff, and the proceedings began.

"You are charged with wilful and unlawful trespass on Crown railway property, contrary to the bye-laws of the Durham County Court and its jurisdiction. For the benefit of the court, state your full name, age and address," he loudly and pompously proclaimed, and prompted the first boy in the line. He was decidedly baffled at all this gobbledegook, and just stared back at the bailiff. "Go on, lad! Say your name ...."

He stuttered his way through, and the others followed in turn; some spoke plainly, like Derek and Dennis, others answered quietly, yet others grudgingly, as if they were snitching on someone. Then back to the front of the line, "How do you plead to the charge – guilty or not guilty?"

The first boy was once more perplexed, and the magistrate prompted, "Say 'guilty' or 'not guilty' boy ..."

The startled boy uttered, "Guilty!" and the bailiff moved onto the next. Each, in turn, responded with the same reply.

Then the magistrate asked for the evidence against the offenders, and one of the policemen stepped forward into the witness box. It was DC Jeffries, looking a lot different in his dress uniform. The magistrate asked the officer to begin, and the detective, consulting his black notebook, started to describe five separate, though similar incidents of trespass, stating names, times and places. Three of the crimes each involved two pairs of boys, three boys were together caught in one trespass, and one other was alone.

The magistrate thanked DC Jeffries for his evidence, and said that he could stand down. He turned to the boys saying, "Do any of you have anything to say before we pass sentence?" Once more the line of apprehensive boys had the chance to speak, though all that each could muster was a timid, "No!"

Turning to his left, the magistrate whispered something to two colleagues on the bench who both nodded. He repeated the words to the man and woman on his right – they too nodded their approval.

The magistrate looked back at the court, sat up straight and summed up. "Each boy is found guilty of the charges. The courts have seen far too much of this lately, and we commend the railway police for their ongoing diligence, and continued efforts to stamp it out. We are pleased to be able to promote their accomplishments further, and subject this appropriate penalty. Each boy is fined half a guinea, to be paid to the clerk to the court treasurer – next case please, bailiff."

With that, all of the offenders were dismissed, before being reunited with their parents. Ten shillings and sixpence was a hefty sum, and a lot of money for Derek's dad – almost a day's wages! He was shocked at the size of the penalty – he'd only brought five shillings with him, and would have to return to pay the full amount of the fine after pay day.

*****

Of course, Derek was blissfully ignorant about how such a large fine detrimentally impacted on the, already tight, family budget. But the money to pay the fine had to be found somewhere, and it meant that Derek's dad had to ask for overtime, and make up the shortfall in the week following. Make no mistake, Derek had already been suitably punished – he was told in no uncertain terms, not to play with *that boy Dennis,* and not allowed out of the house for several days, and had lost all small privileges that he had as the eldest child, including treats or small amounts of pocket money.

But Derek was sadly deluded if he thought that the ordeal was over. Even though both he and Dennis were naïve enough not to understand the eventual outcome and repercussions of their actions, they had it pointed out to them, by several adults, that this misdemeanour would remain on police records, and may permanently tarnish their characters and credibility in the future.

The next disgrace followed rapidly. Page six of next day's *Evening Gazette* reported the court appearance. The names of the ten juvenile lawbreakers and their schools were listed, along with a few lines on how the police were clamping down on railway trespass. There was also a short quote from DC Peter Jeffries, on how the safety of youngsters, as well as adults and railway staff was of paramount importance.

If they hadn't already heard on the grapevine, now the whole estate knew of the trespass, the hearing and the fines. Two families were humiliated and shamed. People knew the two names of the local miscreants, and their two schools, which now had their reputations sullied too.

For Derek, personally, there was one final ignominy, which came as a bolt from the blue, in the week following the hearing. By now the new school term had begun, and Derek was in Class 4A, the top stream of the fourth year juniors. It was Friday, the morning for the whole school assembly. The pupils were all seated in their class lines, the teachers were sitting on chairs at the back of the hall, and the headmaster, old Mr. Watkins, was on the stage at the front. When he started holding forth about the importance of staying safe out of school, Derek's ears pricked up. Mr. Watkins continued by saying that his school had been 'totally ridiculed' and 'scandalised' by the actions of one boy. As he went on to give the whole school details of the crime, it became clear to almost all except the youngest who the headmaster was talking about. If it was his intention to humiliate Derek, then he was succeeding, as knowing heads and eyes began to turn towards him. But Mr. Watkins wasn't finished! He named the culprit and ordered him to stand up!

Derek, to his eternal shame, did as he was bid, slowly, sheepishly stood, hands behind his back, head down in a vain attempt to avoid two hundred and forty pairs of accusing eyes focussed on him. The tirade continued but Derek heard no more, his mind having already switched off.

The rest of the day was sheer agony. Derek had been humbled and debased by the public reprimand of the headmaster. He'd suffered a deep indignity before his friends and classmates, before teachers he admired and looked up to. Most stayed clear of Derek for the rest of the day and few spoke to him, further worsening the disgrace that he already felt. The stigma of reproach seemed permanent, and it would take a long time before this wound would heal, to regain respect, and be fully accepted back into the fold.

Chapter Four – The Fireworks Club

Even a minor event in the life of a child is an event of that child's world and thus a world event.
Gaston Bachelard, philosopher.

Much of the money that the three friends earned from dubious business exploits was put into their Fireworks Club funds. Their enterprise of returning empty bottles to gain the deposit monies, made a lot of cash and a good proportion of it was invested in the Club. Every now and then, they would add to the fund with some of their pocket money, or from money earned running errands. By the first week in October the boys' totals were healthy, and come Bonfire Night, they'd have more than enough to buy the longed-for fireworks.

It was Mr. Jenson, of Jenson's Hardware shop in Norton Village who'd come up with the clever idea of a Fireworks Club, which by now had been successfully running for the last eight years. It was the hardware store which, as well as tools and DIY materials, sold fireworks to local people for the November 5th celebrations. Mr. Jenson's Club was established as a savings scheme and the fund would accumulate over the weeks and months leading up to Guy Fawkes Night – the customer was then able to claim fireworks to the value of the money saved.

Effectively, it was a mini savings bank. For the customer, it meant that there would be no money worries for buying expensive fireworks on the night. You had to be at least twelve years old, to join the club, and when depositing their first amounts, each boy stood as tall as possible in front of Mr. Jenson. The hardware store owner had looked dubiously at each of them, but in the end, he was glad of the custom and turned a blind eye! For Mr. Jenson though, there was a double bonus; throughout the savings period, he could bank the money, keeping any interest for himself rather than passing it onto his customers; further, he knew that *his* hardware shop was the only one in the district where the savings could be spent on fireworks!

One of the most lucrative earners for Derek, Dennis and Micky was *Penny-for-the-Guy*. With about three to four weeks to go before the big night, enterprising kids would make a Guy Fawkes effigy to go on top of the bonfire. But before it did, it had another important use – to make money! The items required were an old pair of trousers, a shirt or jacket, some string and plenty of old newspapers. The papers were easily found, and the old clothes could be scrounged from home ragbags or moth-ridden wardrobes. Kids who could make the best effigies though, were likely to have the most takings.

The three found what they needed easily enough, and began by stuffing scrunched up newspaper inside the clothes to fill them out, then tied off the ends of trousers and sleeves with string, to stop the stuffing from falling out. When laid flat, the arms and torso could pass for a body, albeit a legless, handless and, most importantly, a headless one! The real art came in crafting the head – some kid's Guys were simply a mask placed over rolled-up newspaper, whilst others just used a turnip or a cabbage pinched from their mam's kitchen. Micky, who was the best artist of the boys, had the task of fashioning the head; using cardboard from a cornflake box, he drew and painted a face, looking, for all the world like the picture of Guy Fawkes in the school history books. He cut out the face and moulded it around a newspaper ball, then added long dried grasses to each side for his hair. The other boys were really impressed, and Derek added his granddad's worn-out flat cap to top it off. The boys were more than happy with their Guy, even though the whole effect resembled a farmer's scarecrow rather than the iconic Gunpowder Plotter!

The next important matters to consider, were where and when to make the pitch for Penny-for-the-Guy. The Guy was sat semi-upright on Derek's bogey, and then ceremoniously towed to the best places to earn cash for the Fireworks Club. The boys would sit, backs to a wall, with the Guy in all his glory, next to them and in full view of admiring passers-by. Sometimes they pitched the Guy outside the Melba Bar, where shoppers might stop for a cup of tea, and in passing, would be asked by the boys to contribute, *"a penny for the Guy."* To the boys, they were inviting people to inspect their handiwork, having made this Guy, then to offer money for allowing them to marvel at the fantastic, artistic creation!

Penny-for-the-guy!
(public domain,beefgravy.blogspot.com)

In truth, they were simply begging! But of course all parties knew this – not just the beggars themselves but those contributing too! Many of them had done exactly the same when they were little – it was an impish, even cheeky, way for kids to scrounge a few coppers to spend on sweets, lemonade or – fireworks!

The same *Penny-for-the-Guy* incantation was chanted to all who passed. Most would simply glance across then carry on, many didn't even bother to look, some would stop and stare, and yet others would pass judgement on the quality of the craftwork itself – some said it was the best Guy that they'd seen all week, but most commented on it being either too short or too fat, or it didn't look like Guy Fawkes at all! Only occasionally and irregularly was a penny forthcoming. Those who did would throw a farthing, a penny, or ha'penny on the cloth placed next to the Guy, and the odd thru-penny bit was very welcome. Unlike other Penny-for-the-Guyers, the friends were cute, and always made a point of saying thank you to anyone who contributed – you never knew ... next time they passed, they might very well bestow another donation to the Fireworks Club!

The boys soon realised where the best places to make their pitch were. The first was Norton High Street – where the village shops were! Of course, they had to choose their times carefully: Saturday mornings were always good, as lots of families, or just housewives, were out shopping at the butcher's and greengrocer's, for the Sunday dinner. If there were too many other kids setting up with their Guys, the boys would move on, and turn left into Leven Road, to where the big Co-op was.

Two other good places were outside the Moderne Cinema, and The Avenue Picture House, just across the road. Here too, it was sensible to choose the best time of day, to solicit as many people as possible. As it cost 1/3d for adults and 7d for children, it meant that there was usually plenty of change and spare coppers about. There were two *houses* each day at the cinemas, and the best times to show off the Guy were between the *houses*, when cinema-goers were queuing for the second *house*, and just coming out from the first film showing, or at the end of the night after the last film was over. At the appropriate times, the boys would move pitches between the two cinemas, to catch the maximum number of punters!

But the most lucrative pitches by far, were those outside the pubs! Once again, timing was paramount. Setting up a pitch outside the *Red Lion* or the *Highland Laddie* as the drinkers went in on a Sunday morning was good, as the men were still fairly flush with some of their last week's wages. Being outside the *White Swan* (known locally as the

Mucky Duck) at two o'clock, when the pub was closing for the afternoon, proved even more profitable! Those who were only slightly inebriated usually found a penny or two to give, but those who were more intoxicated (even *pallatic*!), always seemed to find a thru-penny bit in a trouser pocket, a silver sixpence or even a shilling that appeared surplus to their requirements! It was too late for the boys, but Dennis reckoned that if they'd been able to be outside the pubs when they closed at half past ten, they'd have made a small fortune!

Of course, there were other boys with Guys, and they too knew the best spots. Occasionally there were disagreements about whose pitch it was, or who was there first, but they usually able to work around it, positioning the Guys strategically far enough apart so that everyone could attract some donations. Only sometimes did older boys bully them out of the best places, but they'd always find somewhere else almost as good.

*****

It wasn't just older boys who were a problem when it came to Bonfire Night, but gangs of kids who were, roughly, the same age as the three friends (and some even younger), who were out to steal wood from their bonfire – known affectionately as the *bondy*. The place that they had decided for their bonfire was in Micky's garden. His council house was at the end of a row of terraced homes, and its large garden at the side was surrounded by three-foot-six-inch wooden railings.

The bonfire was positioned well away from the railings and the house, otherwise Micky's mam wouldn't have allowed it. The boys scavenged anything that they could which would burn – old tyres and mattresses, wooden planks, broken wooden furniture, off-cuts, tree branches and logs. They towed their bogies from house to house, to take anything that people wanted to get rid of. A good find would be an old wardrobe, or a battered sofa that would burn for a long time; but transporting large finds back to Micky's garden sometimes proved problematic, and often they needed two, or even three bogies to tow the item.

Gradually, the *bondy* took shape as a classical cone, with long wooden pieces around the outside, pointing skywards, and smaller lengths placed inside, or around the edges. Now, Micky's garden was open to the road, and clearly visible to passers-by; it was imperative that the *bondy* was guarded as much as possible, from local raiders! The boys took turns – two would go out with the Guy, and one would stay on patrol, ready to raise the alarm with a parent if anyone looked suspicious.

It was the Somerset Road gangs, or those from farther away on the Bluehall Estate which were the most likely to raid them, especially on those dark autumn evenings when the nights were drawing in. Rather than collect their own firewood, they'd prefer the easier way and just take someone else's. But the lads' careful plans seemed to work, and as they approached Bonfire Night, they had seen off several attempted raids, and that year lost not a single twig from their bonfire!

*****

The Gunpowder Plot celebrations fell on a Thursday. That week also happened to be the schools' half term holiday, or spud-picking week as it was called locally – this was the time for the farms' late season potatoes to be lifted and collected. The boys welcomed the last few days before the big night to beg more Penny-for-the-Guy money, and to make final bonfire preparations. Derek had planned to collect his fireworks from the club on the morning of Wednesday 4th, so that he'd have a good variety to choose from before the rush came. Dennis and Micky had already chosen their fireworks, and pressed him to go to the shop soon. But his plans were scuppered when his mam informed him that he was to look after the baby, whilst she took his sisters and brother to the doctor's clinic in Stockton. He was upset but didn't protest; instead, he decided that after they'd gone, he'd put the baby in the big pram, and take it with him to the hardware store. He knew that during the walk the baby would nod off, as it always had a mid-morning sleep.

The plan worked a treat, even though he had to walk right up to the Green before the baby fell fast asleep. At the hardware shop, he raised the hood of the pram and applied the brake, positioning it outside the front window, where he would have a clear view of it. Derek had made his final club deposit the previous Saturday, and then there were no fireworks to be seen on sale anywhere in the shop, but this day, the shop was absolutely bursting with them! If Derek wasn't excited enough before, now he was completely agog at the Aladdin's Cave full of treasure, before his eyes.

The counter was now a huge glass case, packed with all manner of brightly coloured Standard Fireworks; the shelves behind and at the sides had been cleared for a myriad of Brock's Fireworks selection boxes of all shapes and sizes, each individually priced. Rockets from four feet tall to eighteen inches high, stood vertically stacked behind the counter. A smiling Mr. Jenson, the Firework Wizard himself, stood behind the counter, watching Derek's delighted face and allowing him take it all in!

The Wizard asked Derek for his savings card. The bottom line said twelve shillings and eight pence. Looking around, he saw that the dearest and biggest box in the shop cost a whopping one pound seventeen and six – more than three times the amount that Derek had. It didn't matter though, as Derek wanted to choose his own individual, loose fireworks, and anyway the boxes only had a few (though each one was quite expensive) fireworks inside.

As he selected from the large glass case, Mr. Jenson placed them in a paper carrier bag, and totted up the price as they went along, after each choice. He had to have *Bangers* of course – he chose half a dozen smaller ones at 1½ d each, and another ten *Cannons* at 2d each. Next were the *Jumping Jacks*; these were like *Chinese Firecrackers* that had several cracks and bangs – just the thing for giving the girls a fright! He also needed *Sparklers* – the small sized packets were good enough – some silver and some multi-coloured. Boxes of *Coloured Matches* would be pretty, and good for lighting fireworks too!

Rockets were a must, and Derek chose three smaller ones, and one of medium length. The rest of his savings were spent on a selection of fireworks of various types and sizes – some *Roman Candles*, a couple each of *Silver Rain Fountains* and *Golden Rain Fountains*, three multi-coloured *Volcanoes*, two *Waterfalls* and two *Catherine Wheels* – even though he knew that these wouldn't always spin on the nail!

*****

Derek was beside himself with excitement, and completely elated at finally having these wonderful gems in his possession. He grasped the carrier bag, thanked Mr. Jenson, shot out of the shop and took off home so that he could inspect, touch and even smell, his newly acquired and prized assets. He'd store them in the wash-house, where they'd be safe and secure, and ready for the big night.

He was three-quarters of the way home when he stopped dead! The baby! He'd forgotten the baby! Utterly panic-stricken, he turned tail and bolted straight back to the hardware shop. Fear and dread surging through him - soon he was running, then sprinting at the terrifying thought that he'd lost his baby sister to some kidnappers!

His heart leapt as he turned the final corner and saw that the pram was still there, exactly where he'd left it. Still in a frenzy, and gasping for breath, he gingerly peered under the pram's hood, to find his sister unmoved, and still sleeping peacefully. Dripping with sweat and relief, Derek secreted his fireworks under the baby's mattress, and slowly pushing the pram, set off for home.

*****

The brothers and sisters, mams and dads all came to the bonfire, whilst others watched from the road or from bedroom windows. The Guy, which had done such sterling work, was ceremoniously given pride of place on top of his funeral pyre. The days before had been dry and the bonfire set alight easily – it was bitter-sweet for the lads to see the Guy, made almost entirely of paper, cremated in less than a minute. The three boys pooled their fireworks, and the families added a few more too. Some were disappointing, like the *Catherine Wheels*, which positively refused to spin despite the prodding and cajoling. Some were duds, not going off at all, or lasting just seconds. The younger kids though, were thrilled at being able to hold and wave shimmering *Sparklers*, but best of all were the *Rockets*, each giving a fine display, and getting plenty of loud 'Oooh's and 'Aaah's from the crowd.

As the bonfire dwindled, and bedtime beckoned for the younger ones, people drifted off.

The three were allowed to stay, and roast spuds in the glowing embers – what a treat, even though they were only cooked on the outside, and even if it almost burned the skin off the tongue! Later, they'd add the old armchair, which would probably smoulder 'til morning. The pals had kept a few of their *Bangers*, and when all was quiet they let some off! It was Micky who first had the idea, then they all couldn't help wondering what would happen if ….

Half-asleep, next morning, Micky's mam was at first curious, then furious when she paid a visit to the outside lavatory … how on earth could their porcelain pan have acquired a ten-inch crack right down the middle …?!!

Chapter Five – Messages

A mirror reflects a man's face, but what he is really like is shown by the kind of friends he chooses.
The Bible, Proverbs 27:19.

It was called 'going on a message', and it meant running an errand, or doing a service for someone. It was youngsters with a bit of 'gumption' who were usually chosen – that's to say someone old enough to appreciate what they had to do, and who could be sensible and trustworthy enough to carry out the task well. Derek was pleased that people thought well enough of him to be asked to complete a 'secret operation', but it wasn't exactly Derek's favourite thing to do – he'd much rather play out with his friends, just like other ten-year-old boys. It did, though carry the added incentive of possibly having a reward at the end of the mission!

Whenever his mam asked him to go on a message, he knew it wasn't going to be much fun, and he'd be bored and tired when he returned from the shop, or got back from helping granny. Like it or not, and as selfish as he was, being the eldest of five kids, he knew that it was incumbent on him to help his mam, dad and family in any small ways that he could. Lord knew, they'd told him so often enough!

Derek had very little idea of the real hardship and poverty that his parents had suffered in the wartime years, more especially these last few years, bringing up a large family on the meagre earnings of a father, state child benefits and welfare, and the small handouts that Derek's grandparents could afford.

When Bill and Kitty had married, Bill had only just left the Merchant Navy where he'd been trained as a ship's cook. Like many young couples with no assets, they lived at home with parents, first at Bill's mam and dad's in Norton, then settling at Kitty's mam's in Myrtle Road, in Primrose Hill near Stockton, where Kitty had grown up. They'd put their name down for a council house, but in the 1950s they were in short supply and the housing list was long. They found themselves well down the list, as priority was given to those with children or had nowhere else to go. Eventually, after Derek was born, they were able to have a place on their own, moving to a house on a new council estate in Roseworth.

During all of this time, and since the navy, Bill had a variety of jobs. Derek's birth certificate described his father's occupation as a 'general labourer,' meaning that whilst not having a particular skill, Bill turned his hand to any aspect of manual work that he could comfortably manage. There was no doubting that he was an intelligent man – as a boy, he did well at school, but was unable to reach his potential, as his own parents couldn't afford to send him to grammar school, even though he'd passed the 11-plus. Without a scholarship, he left school before he was fifteen, and like his father before him, joined the Royal Navy in the middle of a world war. Whilst he didn't see much active service as a pom-pom gunner aboard ship, during and after the war, he'd spent time in the Far East and Australia.

After the forces, Bill had found work at the Billingham ICI chemical works, before an accident with inhaled chlorine gas forced him to leave and seek employment away from the debilitating factory atmosphere. He worked for several companies as a van or lorry delivery driver, then as a bus driver, as well as other jobs as a 'general labourer' where heavy manual work was not required.

Before having her first baby, Kitty worked too – as a teenager child-minding then as a cleaner, before getting her first 'proper' job as a sales assistant at Doggarts' department store in Stockton. She started when she was fifteen in the ground-floor Haberdashery Department, where she was expected to learn all aspects of materials, of sewing and needlecraft, of tapestry and knitting, not to mention getting to grips with and being able to demonstrate the latest Singer sewing machines. Kitty loved the new-found freedom from home and school life, and especially meeting new people – young women of her own age, as well as older superiors who brought an order and discipline to her life. She was soon delighted, after good reports from them, when she was given promotion two floors to the women's Lingerie and Underwear department!

Later in life, as one of her party-pieces, Kitty would often tell the story of her first day at Doggarts'; along with Kitty – her maiden name Doreen Onions – there were two other young women starting work – Miss Veronica Leek and Mrs. Peggy Lamb. On hearing each of their names, the senior floor manager on Haberdashery quipped – "Ah, so ladies, we have Miss Lamb, Miss Leek and Miss Onions – now we only need Miss Carrot and we could make an Irish stew!"

*****

Going on messages to the shops for his mam might earn Derek a penny, if his dad had had a good week. Usually there wasn't any reward, Derek didn't expect anything, and didn't ask; if he got a penny or two, then it was a bonus. Sometimes she told Derek that he could spend a ha'penny on sweets for himself, and a ha'penny could buy quite a lot! A small Gobstopper was a good buy, so was four liquorice Jumping Jacks, or a small sugar lolly. If he could chew on a twig of aniseed whilst carting home the bread and potatoes, it would ward off the boredom of completing the tiresome chore.

His Granny would always give Derek a thrupenny bit, from the jar on the top shelf in the kitchen, for running a message. He did love going to his grandparent's house, although he always found it a little intimidating, and somewhat foreboding. There were net curtains on all of the sash windows; there was a valance, with dark, heavy-set drapes hanging at each side – almost like black-out curtains which had been there since the war. There was a wooden sideboard displaying photographs in ornate frames. The only sound in the place came from the prized, oak-cased grandfather clock in the corner, perpetually tick-tocking, and echoing through the whole house.

The living room, looking onto the back-garden allotment reeked with the dense stench of granddad's *Golden Virginia* pipe tobacco. Years of yellow tar had clung to a high ceiling and the once-white, flowery wallpaper. Against the back wall was a dark, mahogany Welsh Dresser displaying a porcelain tea set and cheap Willow Pattern dinner plates. It contrasted with the ebony surround mirror, hanging above the hearth and fireplace, and the bare, stained floorboards which were partly covered by a threadbare carpet.

On the mantelpiece sat a Napoleon clock, with mock-Wedgwood figurines of Victorian ladies at either end. The floor space was filled with granddad's rocking chair and two huge armchairs with matching settee, all of which had seen better days.

Granny's house was down the bank, then up Waterford Road. Derek didn't especially like going past Somerset Road, as there always seemed to be some rascals, like the Hyndmarche kids, hanging about and looking for trouble. Granny's messages were almost always for the same thing, which was to shop for her tipple of choice – two bottles of Newcastle Amber Ale!

The Anchor Wine Lodge outdoor off-license wasn't allowed, by law, to sell alcohol to ten-year-olds, but Granny was a good customer, and had a 'certain arrangement' with the landlady! Anyway, she'd always write a note for Derek, telling the proprietor what she wanted, and then she signed it – which, somehow, seemed to make it all legal!

*****

The best message-tipper though, was Mrs. Williams who lived next door in Clarendon Road. She was a middle-aged woman who lived with her grown-up son Frank. Derek hardly ever saw Frank, though he sometimes heard him rowing with his mam. He worked six days a week, and was out drinking most nights. Occasionally, he glimpsed Frank leaving early for work, or returning late in the evening, staggering home after a night out. Mrs. Williams spent most of her time indoors, invisible behind the net curtains, and only appeared if she needed a message doing. If she was desperate, she'd knock on Derek's door and ask his mam if he could run a message for her. Normally though, as soon as Derek left the house, she'd mysteriously appear and call him over.

Mrs. Williams liked to keep it hush-hush, but Derek's mum knew what sort of message it was, and said nothing. Unless he was just off for a game of footy with the lads, Derek was happy to comply, because even though running the message was a dangerous mission, it could also be very lucrative! Invariably, she wanted Derek to go to the bookie's and place a bet for her – what's more, she would pay Derek a whole shilling for his trouble! To reward him to this extent, Derek thought that Mrs. Williams must be pretty well-off; either that or Frank gave her a good slice of his wages – or that she was a regular winner on the dogs or horses! Strangely though, Derek was never asked to collect any winnings – either there were none, or she picked up the money herself.

Mrs. Williams would select her horses from lists of runners and riders in the *Evening Gazette* the night before. She wrote down the wagers, and gave Derek the money – sometimes half a crown, sometimes five shillings, and if she was really flush, a ten-bob note. Derek had to make his way to the bookies, half way to Stockton, and then surreptitiously watch the men coming and going from the shop.

He had to choose someone that he knew, or looked trustworthy, and then ask if he would place the bets for Derek, as he was too young to be allowed in. He would start to get fidgety if the man was in the shop a long time, fearing that they'd run off with the cash. On acquiring the betting slip, he had to deliver it to Mrs. Williams and received one shilling - easy!

*****

With his new found, and for now regular, income, Derek made the decision to begin saving his earnings, with a view to purchasing something that he'd been craving for several months Dennis already had one, and Micky had been promised one for his birthday; but there was very little chance that Derek's mam and dad could afford to buy him a bike any time in the near, or even distant, future. Pity, as it would have been ideal to go off with his pals, as well as for doing messages more easily and quickly.

He secreted the money in a small 1953 Queen Elizabeth Coronation biscuit tin, and hid it on the top of the wardrobe in the bedroom. Over the weeks, with help from Mrs. Williams, his savings rapidly accumulated, until he had over eleven shillings. It seemed like fate played its hand, when Nobby Clarke asked the lads playing footy in the street to spread the word that he was selling his bike, and anyone who was interested should let him know.

Nobby was two years older than him, and just starting to grow taller and put on some weight; Derek realised that he must be outgrowing his lovely racing bike, but barely gave it a second thought, realising that it would be far too dear for him. With its racing wheels and handlebars, slim saddle and a set of four Sturmey-Archer gears, it was a very good bike; but a nagging curiosity got the better of him. The next time that he saw Nobby, he inquired as to how much he wanted for the bike, as his uncle said that he was going to buy him one!

It was a small white lie, but Derek didn't want anybody to know that he had money to spend; expecting the purchase price to be at least three pounds at the very least, Derek was amazed when Nobby replied, without any hesitation, said that he needed ten shillings to go towards the purchase of a brand new bike.

At this, Derek was also unhesitating, and after viewing and test-riding the bike, without further dilly-dallying, (except for a little haggling) the deal was done for eight shillings. The very same afternoon, Derek and Dennis were riding off together up to the Green, with Dennis expounding relevant parts of the Highway Code, and teaching Derek the rudimentary elements of road-craft.

A racing bike.
(public domain, therustybicycle.blogspot.com)

The bicycle proved to be a good buy in many ways; first, even though eight bob was a lot to pay, what Derek got for his money was very good value! Next, he was pleased to see that his father approved, and that he was clearly impressed his son's good business sense. Thirdly, the new acquisition proved to be a big asset when doing messages, although he did have to figure out how to manage and balance his bike with shopping bags on both handlebars!

What Derek didn't realise at the time, was just how much adventure he would have with this bike, or the many places that it would take him to. He did get cross though, when he occasionally found his bike missing because his dad was late for work and had nabbed it for the day!

Derek wasn't entirely insensitive to the needs of the family, and as the eldest, more and more began to feel as though he should somehow do more to help his mam and dad. He was well aware that the family were far from being well-off by local standards, and in comparison to those of his relatives and his school friends. His father Bill, worked hard as a 'general labourer', but a manual worker's pay was substantially lower than that of an office worker or other white-collar staff.

He supplemented his wages with overtime work, which meant that he was often away from home for long hours of the day. Welfare benefits helped, with child allowance proving to be an absolute godsend. Bill himself wasn't a well man; he'd suffered from a nagging and recurring duodenal ulcer for some years, and a lifetime of smoking cigarettes meant that his weakened lungs were susceptible to regular bouts of chest infections and bronchitis, especially severe in the cold winter months.

There were clear signs when the family's financial budget was stretched to the limit. There'd be far less food around, and bread and potatoes were much more in evidence than fruit and meat. Derek's mam would always eat like a bird so that her husband and children wouldn't go short. There were few sweets or treats for the kids, and any new clothes or shoes would invariably be hand-me-downs from kind friends or caring relatives. More often, laid in bed, Derek would hear raised voices from the living room below, arguments that were clearly about money or, at least, the lack of it.

They couldn't always afford coal for the fire; it was the staple fuel, which kept the whole house warm through the winter, and heated the water through the back-boiler behind the fireplace. Coal and coke were scrounged by his Derek's dad from railway sidings, and wood off-cuts and logs were scavenged from factories and nearby copses.

His mam had packed up smoking some time before, and now dad was reduced to just a few tabs a day. One cold, and wet Autumn night, his dad had given Derek the family's last few coppers, and sent him out on his bike to the off-license to secretly buy a packet of five Woodbines. When Derek returned, soaked to the skin, his mother somehow got wind of what was going on, and a massive argument ensued, based around how Bill was being so selfish, spending their last few pennies on fags, when there were hungry kids to feed. As his dripping wet son skulked quietly away, lest he should be dragged into the row, he saw Bill curse, with anguish and fling the whole packet onto the open fire.

*****

Any money, however small, that Derek earned and could give his mam was very welcome. During the better times, Derek would save most of the coppers that he earned, but when things were tight, and every penny counted, then he'd hand over almost all of his messages money. The new bike allowed Derek to do any messages much more quickly. It was always an annoyance to him though when he'd go to collect it from the wash-house and find it missing – commandeered once more, by his dad to go to go to the bookies. Like smoking, gambling was another of Bill's weaknesses. Not that he wagered a lot – not since the navy did he have the money for that. He enjoyed a flutter on the horses, on Littlewood's football pools or on the dogs. The stakes were paltry, and on the few occasions that he was successful, the winnings weren't nearly enough to radically alter the family's financial situation.

Belle Vue Dog Track, in Norton, had greyhound racing twice a week – Wednesday and Saturday. They all knew someone who had a greyhound, normally the most placid of dogs. Whenever you were out and about, you'd always see someone walking a greyhound. They needed exercising every day, and a sprint or two in the park. Bill took his son with him to a meeting one Saturday night; Derek remembered how packed it was, and his dad had said that they'd come to see one of the best racers that they'd ever had – the course record-holder, *Royalty*.

Going to the dogs! c.1955
(public domain, easyart.se)

He remembered the vivid white track lights, the cries of the bookies shouting the odds, and the excited yelps and cheers of the punters as the traps opened and the race unfolded. He loved the raw speed and the sheer athleticism of the greyhounds as they rounded the turns. He could see what his father loved about it, and ... yes... *Royalty* was his dad's only winner that night ... albeit the short priced, odds-on favourite!

Chapter Six – Rag & Bone Men

> *There are only two lasting bequests we can give our children. One of these is roots; the other, wings.*
> William Holding Carter Jr., writer.

You could do a lot with a few rags in those days. Even the most threadbare tank-tops, un-darned socks and shiny bottomed trousers had a value. The problem was getting your hands on them.

In Derek's family, there weren't that many items of clothing that could become rags; as Derek, the eldest, grew out of his clothes, which were once new or newly knitted, they were passed down to the next eldest of the brothers and sisters. They might even have been passed on to a cousin living in the next street. Little was wasted, and much was recycled – as many times as possible - until the garment had completely given up the ghost – either too stretched or too faded, either shrunk or past patching or darning! Even then, the item wasn't thrown away, rather relegated to the ragbag where it would await a further reincarnation.

The ragbag contained clothing items made mostly from cotton, some things were of terylene or nylon like curtains or sheets, yet others from wool like jumpers and cardigans, scarves or gloves. But woollen things in the ragbag were rare, as they were usually commandeered into service by any knitters in the family; the woollen clothing was unravelled, separated into its various colours, then rolled up into balls in readiness for re-knitting into scarves, baby mittens or baby cardigans.

These knitters tended to be grannies, maiden-aunts or mothers whose families were long grown up – all of whom had plenty of time on their hands and would happily knit away through long winter nights in front of a coal fire, whilst listening to the Light Programme's *Sing Something Simple* on the wireless. Grannies were the worst – rather than buy a new skein of wool to knit, they could smell-out and acquire a discarded cardigan in a ragbag from fifty yards!

It was time to get rid of the ragbag when it got too big and started to get in everyone's way. Derek and his pals would, periodically, procure and pool the family ragbags and take them to the scrap yard and have them 'weighed-in'. If they managed to fill two or three sacks, they'd pack them on a bogie, and take them to the yard on Tilery Bank near Stockton. Before they went, the items were sorted into their various materials – woollens and rags – the latter comprised of any other fabric than wool.

Murphy's Scrap Yard not only took fabrics but just about any sort of scrap at all, including metallic items from cast-iron baths to steel motor cars. It would take heavy lead linings and pipes, copper piping and pans and rusty iron gates. The iron and steel was sold on to the steel works in Middlesbrough and Stockton for melting down in the blast furnaces and recycling. Most prized pieces were chrome flashings from cars and brass items from plumbing joints or piping – these could be easily cleaned up and re-used to bring in a good profit.

Whenever Derek and his friends went to the yard, Murphy himself was always there, as he'd always send someone else out with the horse and cart to look for scrap. The formidable figure of Murphy though, always scared the kids! He had never looked any different since the first time that they'd ventured into the yard. He was tall and robust, and if you caught his eye, it always seemed to ask *...what are you looking at...?!* Derek imagined him as the archetypal school bully in days gone by. He looked as though he would never entertain a visit to the barber shop, as his hair was long, always heavily Brylcreemed but completely dishevelled. Murphy's cheeks and nose were a rosy red from being outdoors all day, and his jaw had a dark five-o'clock-shadow.

He wore a collarless shirt and a colourful bandana tied loosely around his neck. He was squeezed into a black donkey jacket which had leather patches along the shoulders and at the elbows. His dark pants covered an ample waist, and each trouser leg had a piece of string tied below the knee. (Dennis said that it was to stop the yard's rats from running right up his trousers!) His feet and ankles were covered by Wellington boots, which had their tops folded over and outwards.

The yard itself was half tarmac, half mud! Everywhere there were piles of junk, each haphazardly arranged and awaiting their fate. Perhaps only Murphy knew what each mound contained and where he wanted it. He barked orders to two other, smaller men, dressed in similar garb, who scurried about doing his bidding, and seemingly moving each stack in turn to a new place, where it then was piled up again!

There was an area for dismantling cars with a shed next to it for storing the spare parts; there was a great stockpile of used tyres, then a vehicle crushing plant beside the finished articles of large cubes of flattened metal. There was a small crane, with joists and hoists next to it, and further back some offices, a jumbo weighing machine and sacks of clothes and fabrics casually strewn around it.

Murphy first scrutinised each bag to see what type of material it contained. He said nothing to the boys, and they didn't dare to open their mouths. He grunted as each bag was weighed, and pencilled something on a scrap of dirty paper. He disappeared into the gloom of an office, and the lads were left to wait, and eagerly anticipate their reward.

Murphy condescended to speak to the group for the first time. "One and six for the wool and fourpence ha'penny for the cotton," he grunted, handing over the coppers to the nearest boy. Disappointment was inevitable, and the boys felt somewhat short-changed, but as Murphy held each of them with that steely stare, none of them felt brave enough to challenge him, and grudgingly accepted the cash then trudged out of the yard.

*****

Nobody quite knew where the Lightowlers lived – somewhere down Somerset Road, with others under the Fuzzy Bridge in Ragworth. Eddie, the head of the family liked to keep it that way. There was a wife, a granddad and granny, a married daughter with a baby, and sons of various ages from teenagers to toddlers. Eddie and the older teenage lads signed on to the dole every week. On top of that he did a bit of this and a bit of that – anything or any scam that would make a bob or two. Eddie wasn't averse to a bit of hard work mind, and had a finger in a lot of money-making pies, including a window cleaning round, a bit of gardening for those who could afford to pay cash, up Junction Road way; even a bit of handy-man housing work for the council was fine. What's more, he'd always have one or more of his sons in tow to do any heavy lifting work. Whenever the fair came to town you could be sure Eddie and the lads would be at work on the *Waltzer* or the *Dodgems*.

One of Eddie's main earners was collecting scrap, and then selling it to people like Murphy, or to someone else where he might get a better price. Hence Eddie was known locally, and to one and all, as the rag-and-bone man. He had his own cart with the legend *E. Lightowler and Sons* brightly emblazoned on the sides and back. It was harnessed to a large, brown and white, blinkered horse with the unlikely name of Neddy! At night Neddy was tethered and grazed on the common land under the railway bridge, and by day he trotted the streets of Norton, Stockton and Billingham with Eddie or his sons.

Eddie's cry could be heard long before he appeared, giving people the chance to organise anything that they were throwing out. His sing-song voice shouted out for scrap of any sort that tenants wanted to get rid of, and were grateful for someone like Eddie to take it away. The kids could never quite make out just what Eddie was shouting – to most it was ..."Ee-yang-bo," ...which listeners interpreted as ...*Do you have any rags and bones to give away?* ...which always seemed peculiar as he never *did* collect bones! His other cry was ..."Ee ol' ine"... this one at least seemed to make a little more sense, and a bit easier to translate as ...*Have you any items made from metal that you don't want?...*

Rag-and-bone man, c. 1955
(public domain, pinterset.com)

Normally the scrap was given and taken for free, and only occasionally did Lightowler pay a small, and negotiated, amount of money for an item which both parties realised would be worth something more when weighed-in or sold on. If the kids brought a bag of rags, Eddie gave them a balloon, and if they brought a few bagfuls, they'd earn a goldfish, which he caught from a big tank at the back of the cart, and given in a large cellophane bag with water. For the child, it was great to have a new pet, but the mam or dad, without a bowl, always had the problem of where to keep it.

A favourite with the kids, and a good money-spinner for Eddie Lightowler was his Penny-a-Ride. Eddie had the ludicrous idea of attaching a rowing boat to the back of his cart, behind Neddy, and then towing it around the streets to give rides in! The boat itself was a large wooden one, about eight yards long and almost three yards wide. It had wooden planks for seating set across the width of the interior. Eddie had cut a piece of the side out, and put on hinges and a latch to make a door. You could take one step up, walk in through its gate and choose your plank bench.

There was space enough for about thirty children, plus a few adults who weren't quite as trusting of Eddie's safety precautions! There was bunting and flags hanging along both lengths of the boat and from a makeshift mast, with balloons tied fore and aft. On the outside the wooden slats had been painted in rainbow colours, and the inside was left as natural wood and glazed. The entire boat was fastened tight on the cart, which could be pulled by harnessing it to the horse. Who knew how or where the enigmatic Lightowler acquired it, or when the boat last saw water?

Everyone knew when the Penny-a-Ride was coming, because Eddie rang a large hand bell, as he looked for a good place to stop, and wait for the children to turn up. The children were given time to dash home to ask for a penny from their mams, or to grab a small bag of rags, as this would also get them a ride.

Eddie was on the cart with the reins to the horse, and he would collect the rags, whilst one of his sons was on the boat, collecting the pennies and seating everyone. When the boat was full, Neddy would trot off on a short circular route, which he seemed to know by heart. At the front, Eddie looking for all the world like some sort of latter day Pied Piper, would continue to ring his bell to get everyone prepared for the next trip. Those in the boat waved and giggled, as bystanders shouted and waved back at them or even ran alongside cheering.

For most kids, a bike ride or Shanks' Pony were just about the only modes of transport. The occasional holiday bus ride was exciting enough, but to be pulled by a horse - whilst sitting in a boat - was absolutely thrilling, sheer heaven and all for a penny!

Chapter Seven – Jobs for the Boy

Youth is a wonderful thing. What a crime to waste it on children.
George Bernard Shaw, writer and playwright.

As a youngster, there were occasions when Derek would go with his dad to work. It was usually in the school holidays or at weekends; one reason for him going was to get him out from under his mother's feet, especially when plenty of other brothers and sisters started to appear. It was never the 'take-your-child-to-work' for a social and educational experience, like the fashionable trend of the early 21st century, rather an act of unburdening an overwrought mother at home when it wasn't unusual to have four, five or more bairns to look after, as well as a husband 'to do for.' It was an age when the norm was for the female to remain at home as a housewife, and the male to hunter-gather, and sometimes even if there were no children in the marriage.

Derek 'helping' his dad, 1956.

His dad Bill, had many jobs, but most meant manual labouring, or being a van or lorry driver of some type. For Derek, of course, the experience was absolutely wonderful – to be able to leave a sometimes insular and humdrum existence, and to sample some of the fascinations of the world of adults – as the young Derek saw it, to travel the world! He couldn't go with his dad on some of his occupations, but as he got older was expected to help as much as he was able at home or running errands. When Bill drove single and double-decker buses, for example, he couldn't go with him as there was only a single space for the driver, whilst the conductor or conductress would manage the passengers, the bells and collect the fares.

It was the times when his dad was a van or lorry driver that Derek got to go with him. One of Bill's jobs that Derek was physically able enough to help, was that of a collection and delivery driver for the Moderne Laundry in Norton.

Now, in the fifties, there wasn't much of a variety of materials, natural or man-made, for making cloth and clothing, and it was less than usual for most households to have a washing machine, let alone something like a modern-day fully plumbed-in automatic washer-drier. Some might have a single washer, or a Hoover Twin Tub or similar, to wash and spin, but most would hand-wash or poss-tub wash, then wring clothes out by hand or with an old mangle, and finally dry them on an outside line, before ironing.

Some houses, especially terraces, had external outhouses, or washhouses, specifically for these chores. Those who were more well-to-do might use a self-service launderette where large automatic machines would wash, rinse and even dry clothing; others might take their clothes to a dry-cleaner, or send items to an industrial laundry, like the Moderne.

For Bill, the process involved collecting the 'bagwash', taking it to the laundry, and then returning it a week later. The bagwash was having items cleaned at the low winter tariff – the clothes and materials were collected in a cotton or linen bag, and returned fully cleaned, dried and folded, with a clean new bag for the following week's wash. Costlier, but higher quality services were offered, where clothes and sheets would be pressed and coats, suits and silks could be dry-cleaned. Customers paid Bill, mostly with cash, on the return of washing; some, like a boarding house manageress, would have an account which was settled-up at the end of the month.

Derek's part in it all was minimal, mostly fetching and carrying small parcels of laundry to someone's house where he might receive a sweetie for his trouble, but he handled no money – that was looked after by Bill who kept an accounts ledger and collected all of the payments. The thrill for Derek was being able to go off in a van, with his own passenger seat, and travel to seemingly exotic and faraway places like Billingham, West Hartlepool, North Ormesby and Cargo Fleet!

Derek's dad, Bill.

Bill didn't have the same vehicle every day. The vans themselves were fairly basic for driver and passenger; there were only two hard seats in the front, the sweet smell of cleaned laundry pervaded the whole of the cab. There were no seat belts and both of the windows were manual wind-ups.

Just about the only things on the dashboard were a speedometer, a choke and a couple of switches for lights and the windscreen-wiper. Engines were low in power, and gearboxes basic. Some had column gear change levers, and some had floor-mounted sticks. The vans spluttered along, and a whole lot of double-declutching had to be performed at the very hint of a rise in the road's gradient.

But for Derek – well, he was king of the road; his family, like most, didn't have a car, and travelling any distance normally meant hoofing it or riding the top deck of the bus, preferably in the front seat.

In this early introduction to the world of work, for Derek, meeting people was an added bonus. They were mostly professional people; they were generally those whose social and financial status were on a higher standing than his own and of his family. Even so, that didn't necessarily dictate whether he thought that they were, either good or bad people. Despite many being as nice as pie to Derek, a child, he didn't exactly take to anyone with high or mighty ways, who would try to take advantage of his father's good nature, or verbally abuse him over the size of the laundry bill. But most he found to be good and ordinary folk, kind and courteous people who, like everyone else, were just striving to make as good a living as possible.

But the favourites were his dad's friends and colleagues at the laundry. They seemed to be a sanguine and genuine bunch always with the usual greeting of *Ow do!* or *Away man!,* always chirruping and taking the micky out of each other. Derek even liked the rowdy laughter though he rarely understood the jokes! He liked it, and reddened when they passed comment about him, or some young, blonde lass ruffled his hair, or forced him to accept a blackcurrant Spangle.

One Saturday afternoon in the winter of 1958, Bill and Derek were just finishing the shift, and returning to the laundry depot via Norton Road. There were just a few cars passing. It had been a miserable day weather-wise, raining almost continually since mid-morning from heavy, dark clouds. They were both wet and tired, and looking forward to getting home. As they passed Tilery Rec, they saw a few people gathered in the drizzle, around the small bridge over the Lustrum Beck, which is a tributary of the River Tees. Derek knew the stream, and had played around there and in the rec nearby, with his pals or his mam and brothers and sisters. It was a fairly small brook, about 12 to 15 feet wide at that point, though it could swell to be much wider after heavy rain. Its depth, on average, was two feet at the most, but this day it would be three to four feet in places.

Through the gloom, as they crossed the bridge, they could vaguely see that something was wrong. Bill pulled over and jumped out, and walking back, told Derek to stay in the van. But he couldn't curb his curiosity, and followed his dad back along the pavement. A catastrophic sight greeted their eyes! The bridge's metallic fencing was completely gone, and the pathway lay open to a twelve-foot drop to the beck. When they peered over the edge, they were astounded to see a green double-decker bus laid on its side in the beck. They took in the whole scene very quickly – the bus's engine was off, but it had its lights still on inside and out. There didn't seem to be much damage except for some broken windows and the emergency exit window/door pushed right out and off its hinges. It was eerily quiet except for the pitter-patter of rain, the gently flowing water, the hum of passing vehicles and a few gentle mutterings from below.

The accident seemed to have only just happened a few minutes before. A few others were looking down, whispering between themselves, and gawping over the precipice. The stream was oblivious to the chaos and continued its journey, swirling over, through and around the impotent bus. There were three or four people standing on the left-hand bank of the stream, others sitting on the right side, the uniformed figures of the driver and conductress could be made out lying down but fully conscious. The inside of the bus appeared to be clear and empty.

One man was on his hands and knees frantically assisting the injured driver. He turned his face upwards to the onlookers and, almost shrieking at them, said that they shouldn't just stand there but come down to help him. One young man leapt down to the muddy bank, and an older woman shouted back that she'd phoned 999 and that rescuers were on their way. At that very moment, the ring of the ambulance bell could be heard rapidly approaching from Stockton.

Bill decided that there was nothing that could be done which wasn't already being done – he was no medical man, and the ambulance and fire brigade would be there at any moment. What's more, he had become suddenly conscious of the adverse effect that all of this might be having on his young son, and drew Derek away saying that they should give the rescuers some space.

It appeared everything would be all right, notwithstanding the injured driver of course. Even so, how on earth would they be able to get the stricken double-decker out of the beck, Derek pondered?

The late Monday afternoon edition of the *Evening Gazette* carried the story, exhibiting, on its front page, a stark black-and-white photograph of the bus in the beck. Worse still was the headline –

2 DEAD IN BUS TRAGEDY !

– it screamed out in bold lettering!

A police sergeant had informed the reporter, that the bus had swerved, then due to heavy rain and wet roads, had skidded back again and leaned over sideways so far that it toppled over completely, exactly by the small bridge, over the edge and into the beck, taking the whole of the fencing with it!

The worst, and most pitiful part of the catastrophe, was that a young mother, who had been walking across the bridge at that very same instant, with her baby in a pram, was carried over with the bus, and both were instantly crushed beneath it.

Derek was horrified and even physically nauseous when his father described the article and showed him the photo – the very fact that they themselves had been staring down at the tragedy, and never even realised what lay hidden beneath. Had the shrieking man known? He didn't say – is that why he was so frantic, and adamant that they should go down to help?

It took a long time for Bill, let alone his son, to come to terms with what he'd seen. Was there really nothing they could have done? He believed that there was not, but still felt, well … guilty. What was the probability of the bus swerving and toppling at exactly that point by the bridge …?

Shorter still, were the odds of a mother and child walking along a quiet path, then crossing the bridge at the exact moment that a bus appeared! Bill was a believer in destiny, and he felt sure that fate had played a vital role in the Lustrum Beck bus disaster!

One of Bill's later jobs, when Derek was a teenager, was that of an ambulance driver. By then, Derek wasn't helping his dad, and anyway, he couldn't have helped in that sort of work. In those days, before the onset of skilled ambulance nurses and paramedics, Bill was, basically, a driver, with few medical skills – simply someone who would fetch and carry casualties, the old or the infirm, to and from hospital. But he didn't stay long in that job, he didn't like it, as he told Derek. It scared him, some of the awful things that he saw, things that he didn't think anybody should see. And things that he didn't want to tell his family about, especially at road traffic accidents, when it was left to him to clear away, or collect up body parts, literally with a brush and shovel!

*****

Derek reckoned that his father's favourite job was that of a milkman! As soon as his float was loaded with milks and creams at the dairy, he was his own boss, out and away at the crack of dawn, king of the road for the next few hours at least, his electric cart silently cutting through the early morning mist at a maximum, but impressive, speed of 15 mph! You had to have a driver's licence for a milk float, but trolleys could be operated without – these were electric carts which moved when a long lever at the front was depressed and the milkman, though usually the milk-woman or a younger girl, 'pulled' or towed the float along behind them.

The central distribution Co-op dairy was in the centre of Stockton, and Bill's round was in the posh suburbs of Fairfield and Hartburn. Between 4 and 5 o'clock in the morning, all of the vans, lorries and milk floats were loaded up with crates of creams, yoghurts and all manner of milk types. It must have been quite a sight around five, when scores of vehicles exited the depot into a morning of winter gloom or summer glow.

When Derek was ten, he began to help his father on the round. Mostly, he'd get up later than Bill, then walk, or bus-it to Fairfield for 8 to 9 o'clock in the morning, to help deliver to the doorsteps. Occasionally, on Saturdays usually, Derek would get up early and go to the dairy with his dad, to be with him from the beginning. By midday, the deliveries would be done, and by half past one they'd be home, and dad would take an afternoon nap.

Derek liked the hustle and bustle of work and enterprise at the depot, and seeing and listening to the milk workers. Even early in the day, there'd be some sort of high-jinks going on, with giggling, and jibes being poked at one another. There was always time for good-humoured banter between them, as well as the added fun and chat with the young lasses or women, and extra raucous laughter at some smutty joke or innuendo!

A co-op dairy depot, c.1955.
(public domain, imdb.org)

Bill took his bait for lunch, or rather a late breakfast, as it turned out. He couldn't do without a cup 'o tea, and always took his flask, with at least two sugars per cup. The sustenance was invigorating, and especially welcome and necessary on icy or snowy days. The milk float had no sides, and the cab had no doors, so that there was very little cover and they were completely open to the elements. If the weather was really inclement, there was usually someone who took pity, particularly on 'the little lad', and would invite them in for tea and a biscuit.

One of Bill's problems, and especially after drinking so much tea, was his bladder, and the difficulty of trying to retain the body's waste fluids! Trouble was, there were no public toilets on those new, modern estates, and Bill was loathe to ask customers if he could use their facilities. Consequently, Bill devised and engineered his very own ingenious method of taking a leak! By about 11 a.m. on the round, he had reached the edge of the housing estates. Beyond there were only fields with cattle grazing, and school playing fields – ideal for a peaceful stop and the morning break.

Bill had made a urine receptacle from a Fairy Liquid bottle by cutting the top off and leaving a hole big enough to pee into! In his cab, he'd sneak the bottle down his pants, do the deed and then later surreptitiously empty the contents in the drain by the fields, further along the lane. He had a selection of sizes, the use of which depended upon how desperate he was and how full his bladder was; the small washing-up bottle was fairly useless, the pint size normally adequate, but the large 1½ pint one was just ideal!

The Fairfield / Hartburn milk round was one of the farthest away from the depot. Now, all the depot's milk floats had their batteries recharged every afternoon and night – for at least twelve to fourteen hours every day. Even so, Bill's float was right on the limit of its battery's electrical power; in order to get him out, around the estates, and back home to the depot, he had to go easy on the accelerator. On really cold days, the battery's power seemed to just ebb away, and more than once in winter, he needed to call out the breakdown truck to tow him back.

*****

Derek's dad had always enjoyed a flutter on the horses or the dogs, though he rarely had the resources to win or lose very much money. He liked going to the dogs at Tilery Racetrack, and was always checking the runners and riders at race meetings. He reckoned he had a system – he followed the fortunes of the trainers rather than the horses or the jockeys. He didn't do that much gambling anyway, but the system seemed to let him down, as any meagre winnings were as often as not quickly recouped by the bookies, known better to Bill as *'those robbin' beggars'*!

On his way back from the round, Bill often made a point of dropping into William Hill's in Dovecot Street to check on the latest odds. One time the cart was left outside with Derek to 'mind.' He fancied himself as a driver and would sit himself in his dad's seat, turning the steering wheel and pretending to push the accelerator. It was Saturday, Market Day, and the town was packed. Unnoticed by Derek, a patrolling police sergeant and his constable approached from behind.

'What have we here, a budding Stirling Moss?' the sergeant sarcastically uttered, followed by an

improbable question from the sniggering constable, *'Is this your vehicle sir?'* Derek blushed red, and could do no more than to respond that he was looking after the float for his dad whilst he was in the shop!

Derek was glad to see his dad reappear, but then had to watch and listen as the sergeant tore a strip off Bill, then continued to berate him about leaving an unlicensed minor in charge of a lethal motor vehicle! For his part, Bill was full of *'yes sir,'* *'no sir'* and *'sorry sir it, won't happen again sir'* and he was happy to be on his way again without further penalty. Bill's only comment to his son, when they were well out of sight of the coppers was *'Away man - flamin' rossers – should be out catching some robbers!'*

The Co-op though, treated its customers and workers very well. Customers, every few months, were able to claim *the divvy* – a share of the dividend profits of the Wholesale Society. Everyone had their own *divvy* number and would quote it every time a purchase was made at the stores. Derek, like his parents and siblings, never forgot their number – 56009, pronounced 'five six double-

0 nine' - sang out rhythmically so as to always be remembered! Employees and family members received other benefits from the Co-op too. Each December, Christmas parties were arranged for their children, as well as annual visits to the pantomime at the Globe Theatre in Stockton. Derek always remembered the treat in December 1959, when he saw Cliff Richard *appear in Babes in the Wood.*

Panto in Stockton, December 1959.
(www.stanlaundon.com)

To top it all, at the panto each lucky child received an orange Kiora drink, a chocolate ice cream and a Cadbury's Selection Box absolutely free!

Derek helped his dad on the round as much as he could, and often missed out on going off or playing with his pals. In his second and third years into secondary school, his opportunities to be a member of the school football and cross-country running teams increased. When he was selected, it meant playing or running on Saturday mornings. Derek became torn between helping dad on the round and participating in something that he had become passionate about. If Derek chose the latter, his dad felt that he was being selfish, and made his disappointment obvious, often by silence, sometimes even by shunning his son. Derek felt his father's disgruntlement, and the guilt of letting him down was to hang heavy on him for a long time.

*Bill's second spell as a bus driver with
the Nº. 7 bus at Roseworth terminus, 1967.*

Chapter Eight – Derek at School, Infants & Juniors

 _____

Youth is a wonderful thing. What a crime to waste it on children!
Oscar Wilde, writer and playwright.

Statistics document a distinct rise in the numbers of live births in many Western countries, in the years immediately following the Second World War. In Britain, this 'baby boom' began in 1946, and continued the trend up until about 1950, when it levelled out, before there were later 'booms' in the sixties and again in the eighties. Derek was a baby-boomer, in the first wave, conceived in 1948 and born in February 1949. Derek didn't know that he was a boomer at the time, of course, indeed it was only after the 1951 census that statisticians realised the full extent of the post-war boom and began to wrestle in earnest with its implications.

The rise in the birth rate meant that government, local authorities and councils had to make provision for further education, health and social services improvements, and to retrain work forces. More immediately, they needed to plan for more new housing over and above the already depleted stock due to wartime damage, as well to provide an adequate number of nursery and school places. With plenty of work available in the late forties, de-mobbed soldiers were able to retrain, or find manual labour relatively easily. Some were hastily trained for education and quickly recruited, particularly for the secondary sector, to teach the practical skills that they'd learned in the forces.

By the time that Derek entered the education system, his local authority's schools, like many other areas, were crammed to the rafters with pupils. More teachers were needed, class sizes were bigger and there was a need for additional buildings for classrooms. One solution was to add 'extensions' or hastily build mobile-classrooms; many of these were like post-war prefabs. They were initially meant to be temporary, but remained in permanent use for years to follow. They tended to be cramped spaces, as once the desks and furniture were in, there was little room left for the pupils! Post-war Britain's main priorities lay elsewhere, and especially with the replacement of lost council housing and up grading its aging stock of Victorian and Edwardian accommodation.

Derek was totally oblivious to all the political changes that were happening, after the doldrums of the thirties and forties. Indeed, previous generations before Derek's had lived through two World Wars, and had known nothing but austerity; most found it hard to believe that they had been living through a post-war economic boom, when the then Prime Minister, Harold McMillan told them that they'd "never had it so good"!

*****

Recollecting his early school days, Derek's memories were vague, and in particularly he thought of his infant years as marking time, whilst awaiting something more momentous to happen! Clearly, though perhaps unaware, he was learning – through the three R's as well as developing interactive skills and becoming proficient socially. He wasn't an outstanding pupil, but was clever enough to realise that there were brighter, smarter children than him around, and to keep up he'd have to work just as hard, if not harder.

He recalled feeling pangs of envy about other children. Some appeared to be more confident than him – some came from more affluent families, and others were simply more able to apply themselves better than he could. The braces holding up his short pants didn't help his confidence, nor did the Fair Isle, short-sleeved, hand-me-down tank tops! Being the eldest in his own family of five children, meant that he had no role models to look up, or aspire to, even though his parents were always supportive. Kids born in the early months of the school year, from September to December of 1948, seemed to be so much bigger physically, as well as intellectually more mature, and seemed able to become attuned that much more easily to school life in general. Even so, he in turn felt more superior in outlook and attainment than those who, say, were born in the August of 1949, rather than in February!

The junior school years are those where his earliest major memories come from. Up to then, the classes had been of mixed ability, but streaming was implemented, and the pupils were assessed, when they entered the Junior department. There were two streams in Derek's school, and each of the four year-groups had two classes and all were very full. Some of the bigger schools, like Newtown Juniors, had four streamed classes in each year group! Derek found himself in Junior Class 1B – the lower of the two classes in the first junior year. Its very name already gave almost 40 pupils second-class status. All in all, this did not suit Derek, and he was acutely aware that others were being treated more favourably than him. He wasn't quite sure why he felt the way that he did, even though he realised other children were brighter than him, and it didn't exactly help to promote his self-confidence.

Although the topics taught in each stream should have been of a similar nature, it was inevitable that the ideas and concepts would be pitched lower in the 'B' stream than the 'A', perhaps because some pupils struggled intellectually more than others. Consequently, 'B' stream teachers' expectations were lower. And kids being kids, they knew exactly what was going on, and the 'A's inherently felt themselves superior. Those in the 'A' stream looked down upon those in the 'B' stream, as second-class citizens whose educational capabilities were less than adequate. Friends in the playground too, would come from those in one's own class, despite who your friends had been in the infant classes.

Derek in Class 2B, aged 8

From his point of view, Derek didn't like this state of affairs one little bit, and inwardly promised himself that he'd do his best to change the situation, so that he too could become one of the elite. Of course, the best way to do this was to excel at work, and in particular, succeed at the end-of-year tests.

It worked rather like the professional football leagues; if you finished in the top three, then you were promoted, and sadly if you finished in the bottom three you were relegated.

Your class league position was determined by totalling up your scores for arithmetic, tables, spelling, reading, story-writing and verbal reasoning.

Derek was always destined to be a late developer; at the end of Junior 1, he finished fifth in his class, and it wasn't until the end of Junior 2 that he managed to be promoted to the 'A' stream, by coming second in 2B, in class tests. But then in Juniors 3 and 4, Derek found that he had to raise his game substantially in order to keep up with new found A-Stream friends like Geoffrey Brown and Arthur Price.

It was one thing being on a par with them in playground marbles or British Bulldog, but quite another to compete with them intellectually, or to work at a level where goals and aspirations were considerably higher.

For everyone, some memories of school days are more vivid than others.

Derek was 7 years old when, on June 4th 1956, the entire school was emptied – infants, juniors and all of the teachers – went on an expedition to Norton Green. Everyone was excitedly chattering and waving school-made Union Jack flags as the children walked the three quarters of a mile, two-by-two, in a long crocodile line. They were going to see Her Majesty Queen Elizabeth II, and her husband the Duke of Edinburgh, who were visiting Stockton as part of the monarch's visit to the North East, and to graciously allow her 'subjects' to see her! Everyone from Derek's school was settled on the Green at the appointed time, along with other schools' children who had their positions too.

Plaque commemorating the visit
of Queen Elizabeth II, 1956.

After a few false alarms, finally a cheer went up and flags began to be waved frantically, as the cavalcade of cars approached. Suddenly, there she was – in the back of an open-topped, black Rolls Royce royally waving back to a multitude of screaming school children! She didn't stop though, and no sooner was she there than she was gone, after just a few seconds whisked away down Norton High Street and into Stockton for a civic reception and slap-up lunch with the mayor and lady mayoress.

Derek, like everyone else, was left somewhat deflated and set off on the long traipse back to school; ah well, at least they'd seen the country's monarch, and better still they'd had a whole morning off school!

*****

As well as the core 3R's subjects of reading, (w)riting and (a)rithmetic, study was extending to other areas – most were all right and a few proved challenging to Derek. He liked P.E. (which had only recently changed its name from P.T. – Physical Training) and country dancing. Singing and hymn practice was something he found boring – it was normally completed with four classes – two whole year groups together, and was taken by two of the teachers, whilst the other two 'marked books' or more probably, drank tea and smoked fags in the staffroom!

A similar situation happened on Wednesday afternoons – the whole junior school sat in the big hall to watch one or more short films shown on a huge reel-to-reel projector. They were either government sponsored films or British Film Board educational films on our world, nature or modern trends and the latest breakthroughs in medicine and science. Some were of interest, others above the intellectual level of pupils, and especially those in Junior 3. At the start, all of the teachers were in the hall, and a little while later, after the blackout curtains had been closed, you could look around and see hardly any teachers – strange …!

Derek loved Nature Study, and all the science that went with how the changing of the seasons affected plant and animal behaviour. When he was in Mrs. Gill's class, Junior 4A, they had a science project about the Sun, the Moon and the planets. The project's culmination would be a partial solar eclipse. The day before the eclipse, everyone made small viewers to watch the phenomenon. Mrs. Gill warned everyone never to look directly at the sun, on pain of death, well at least on pain of total blindness. Everybody looked forward to the event, and no-one even considered that it might be cloudy!

Mercifully, the heavens were blue on that autumn day, 2nd October 1959, and 4A and 4B were gathered together on the lawn in front of their classrooms at the appointed hour. They were all armed with their card viewers with pin holes, all looked skywards to see the bright disc of the sun being partly obscured by the dark shape of the moon passing in front of it. They were informed that everywhere would go dark, but were left unimpressed when the daylight only dimmed slightly. Afterwards though, the project became more alive with writing, pictures, sketches and diagrams – they'd all witnessed just a little bit of science history!

For Art and Handicrafts, the year groups split and this time all the boys were together to paint, to construct models with balsa and papier maché, or to make bowls with bamboo and raffia. The girls were instructed in painting, sewing and learning how to crochet place mats or knit scarves for dolls. Generally, pupils sat and worked in silence, and once, when old Mr. Brown was teaching art, Derek was stuck and turned around to watch him showing the boy behind what to do, and he received a smart and hurtful clip around the back of his head!

Derek aged 10 in Class 4A, 1959.

Derek was a quick learner – he never did that again!

There were intense sessions of Handwriting Writing practice, where children sat in silence perfecting the art of Cursive by copying letters and phrases from the blackboard, or copying whole chunks of text from their class reader.

Every day, after dinner, everyone in class would read by themselves, or read a chapter together from the class reader. You shared a book with your neighbour, and everyone took a turn at reading aloud. In Junior 3 they used pencil and paper and in Junior 4 they used ink pens, with changeable nibs and blue/black ink from an inkwell, that had its receptacle in the desktop. Being the inkwell monitor, to make sure all were topped up well, was a very illustrious position and one given only to those most careful and conscientious. After Derek managed to leave a huge blot on one desk and drip ink around the floor of the classroom, he was never required or requested to complete the task again!

The end-of-week spelling and tables tests were something that Derek didn't always look forward to; daily there were spelling bees, where everyone in class had a turn at spelling one of the week's words out loud, and there were sessions when the whole class would chant the tables in unison – *one two is two, two twos are four* and so on. There were whole-class, reading-together sessions when each, in turn, read a few paragraphs aloud.

One of his favourite subjects though was History, especially if it came in story form, like how Queen Boudicca chased the Romans, or King Charles getting his head chopped off! Scripture was also a good source of stories like *The Good Samaritan*, which touched Derek, pricking his inner conscience and raising his spiritual and social awareness. These along with Geography and Map Study were ideal for *doing a topic on*, where you could copy, write and draw to your heart's content.

*****

When Derek and his friends had arrived in classes 4A and 4B, the biggest deal for all of them was sitting the 11-plus. They'd heard all about it from the teachers and older kids throughout all of the previous year. The overall total marks, from two tests to be taken in February of the final junior year, would decide which type of secondary school they would each attend the following September.

The results would be known before Easter of that year and in all likelihood, they'd be split up from many of their friends. They might meet up with some again in September along with other kids from junior schools from all over the town. To go up to the big school was eagerly anticipated, but there were reservations about leaving friends. Taking a leap into the unknown was less than appealing to many, and during the months of waiting, the very concept of change was a frightening one, to parents and pupils alike.

Throughout the Autumn Term, Mrs. Gill drilled her charges in tables, spelling, mathematics, and story-writing, as well as verbal-reasoning and problem-solving. In Class 4B, Mr. Brown did the same with his charges.

It was generally accepted that most of the children in 4A would go to a Grammar School – Stockton Grammar for Boys or Grangefield Grammar for Girls. Most of the pupils in Class 4B were expected to go to a Secondary Modern School – Frederick Nattrass Seniors for the boys, and William Newton Secondary Modern for the girls. Some in 4A and some in 4B would go to Richard

Hind Secondary Technical for Boys, or for Girls - sort of middle-way schools.

The 11-plus tests were taken by all pupils in their final junior year right across the country. There were two parts to the test – Arithmetic and Mental Arithmetic, and Story-Writing and Verbal Reasoning. The latter was, supposedly, some sort of guide to a child's intelligence or intellectual quotient. There was a threshold level to reach, when totalling all of the marks, and the scores would decide whether one would go to grammar school or elsewhere. There was a lower cut-off mark too, below which one would attend a secondary modern school. Those in the 'centre group' would go to the technical schools. It wasn't until years after that educationalists realised that, at the age of 11, not everyone was working at their peak, or even optimum, level – some were more intellectually developed at 12, 13 or even 14 years of age.

Derek, as already stated, was a late-developer physically, emotionally and more pertinently here, intellectually. He 'failed' the 11-plus, or to put it another way, he passed half of the 11-plus, and was destined, in September 1960, to enter the Richard Hind Secondary Technical Boys' School.

Certainly, fate played its hand here – but for the sake of a few extra marks his world may have taken a completely different turn. As much as he remembered his primary school days with fondness and much affection, another phase of his was now about to begin.

Derek aged 11
in secondary school.

Derek aged 13,
Richard Hind school.

Printed in Great Britain
by Amazon